My Time To Color

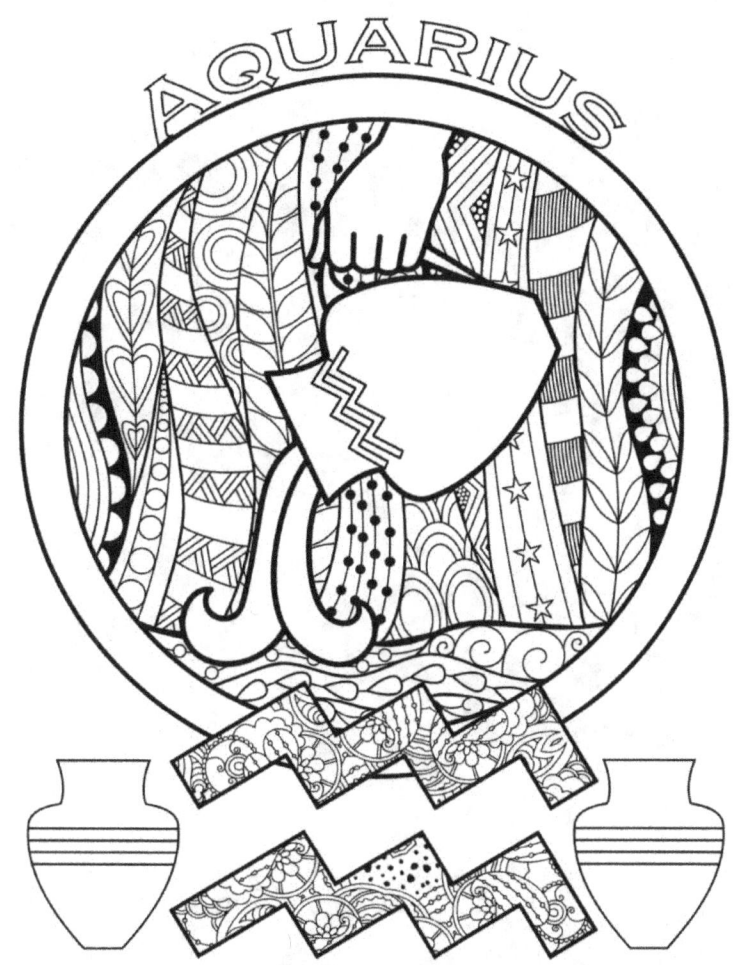

Aquarius Zodiac Sign

Coloring Book

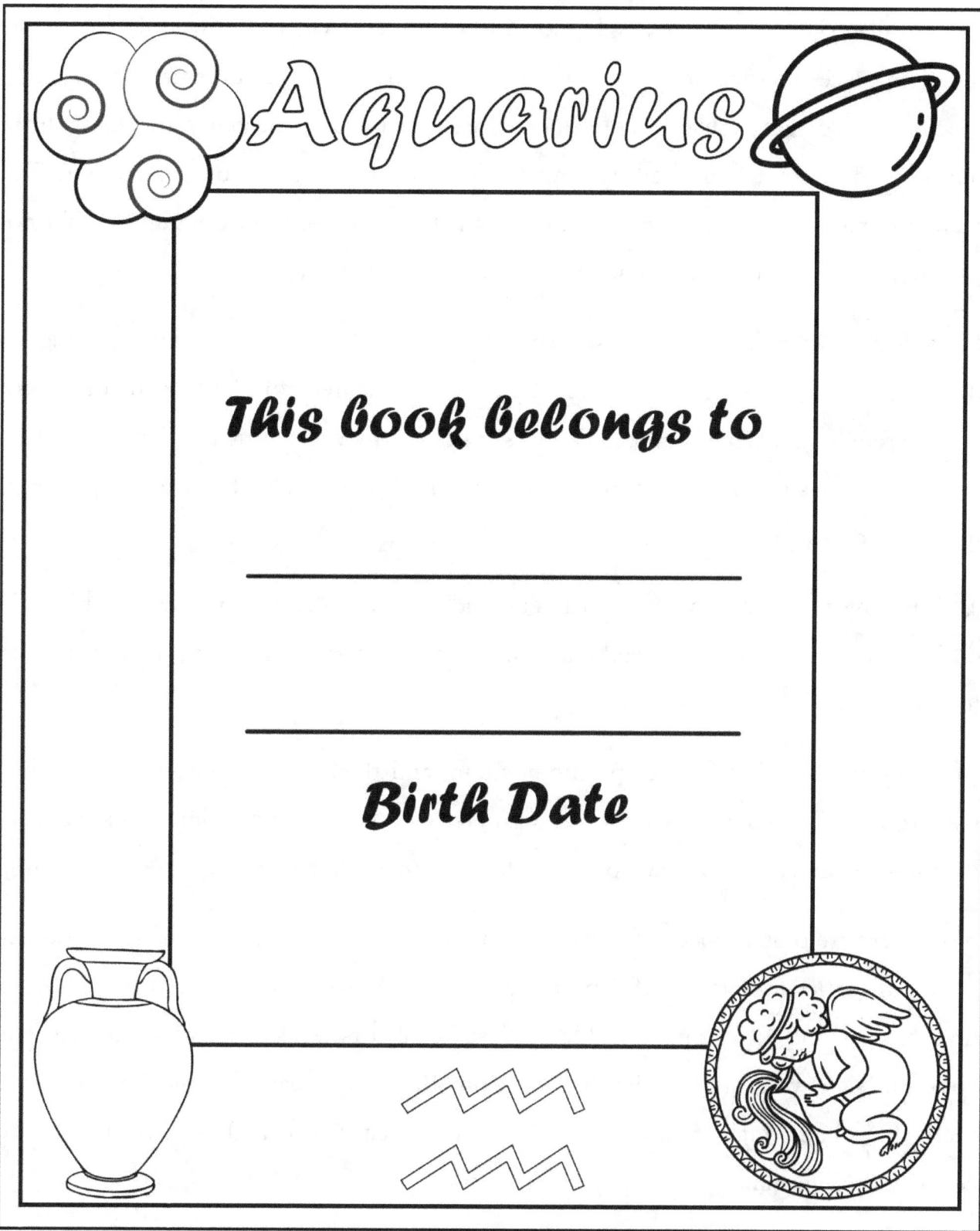

Aquarius

This book belongs to

_____

_____

Birth Date

BORN ON THE CUSP?

Your zodiac sign is based upon the position of the Sun when you were born. At the time and place of your birth the Sun was in a specific position and therefore within a specific zodiac sign. While it would be more convenient if the Sun's transition from one sign to another happened exactly at midnight on any given day, it doesn't. Plus there are many various time zones throughout the world, so your midnight would not be the same as midnight for someone in a different time zone.

In addition, a calendar year is not the same as the Earth's annual revolution (circling) of the Sun. The actual length of a sidereal year (time required for Earth to revolve once around the Sun) is actually 365.25635 days. That is why every four years there is a leap year of 366 days to compensate for the error caused by the calendar year being shorter than the sidereal year.

This is why the Sun can be in different zodiac signs on the same calendar day in different years. The start and end dates of the zodiac signs can and do vary from year to year.

In reality the Sun was in one specific position, and therefore one specific sign, when you were born. Before the age of computers it used to be very time consuming to determine your sign if you were born on the cusp (near the beginning or end of a sign).

Now there are online calculators that you can use to make this determination. You will get the most accurate results if you have all three of these: 1) your day of birth 2) your time of birth and 3) your place of birth. Most calculators will still allow you to calculate your sun sign without your time of birth but the determination could be off. Input these three items into an accurate online sun sign calculator and you will be able to confidently determine your Sun sign.

This web page has an online calculator for determining your sign:
www.MyTimeToColor.com/sign

ZODIAC SUN SIGN AQUARIUS

January 21 to February 19 (* see 'Born on the CUSP?')

Symbol: Water Bearer / Jugs

Element: Air

Quality: Fixed

Ruling Planet: Uranus

Lucky numbers: 2, 3, 7, 9

Color: Turquoise

Favorite Environment: Busy places, Large cities

Governs: Knees to ankles, Circulation

Best Pet: Hamster

Flowers: Amaryllis, Orchid

WHAT IS ASTROLOGY?

Astrology is the use of heavenly bodies to guide us in our lives. It is based on the belief that the stars and planets have a direct impact on our lives and that their relative positions to each other predict certain events. Most people know astrology from their horoscopes and some characteristics of their Zodiac sign, but there is much more to it. You can gain a deeper knowledge of astrology and use it to improve your life.

There are twelve Zodiac signs. Your day and time of your birth determines your zodiac sign. Each Zodiac sign also has a quality, an element, and a ruling planet (or two). For example, if you were born November 14th, (like me!) your sign is Scorpio, your element is Water, your quality is Fixed, and your ruling planets are Pluto and Mars. Each of these pieces of astrological information give you useful knowledge about yourself and how you will interact with people of different Zodiac signs.

History of Astrology

Astrology has a rich history and has arisen independently in many civilizations throughout the centuries. Ever since the rise of humans, people have been observing the stars and planets. Knowledge of these bodies increased drastically with writing to record patterns that took place over long periods of time. Astrology first originated with the Babylonians about 4,000 years ago, when they began to use the stars to predict seasonal and astronomical events.

Since there are 12 lunar cycles in a year, they associated a constellation with each cycle, one that was always in the same part of the sky during that cycle. They then named these constellations after animals and gods. These constellations could be used to tell somewhat reliably what was about to happen with the weather, so we have the stars predicting the future. Astrology! They also believed that when a planet that represented a god gave bad omens, it meant that god was angry. They then attempted to appease it to protect the king and their nation, which meant they believed in a two-way interaction between the movements in the sky and the actions of humans.

The Chinese developed their own system of astrology, with twelve Zodiac signs based on animals representing the years in which they were born, and five elements. Confucius believed in astrology, saying, "Heaven sends down its good or evil symbols and wise men act accordingly." They believed that the stars and planets predicted the rise and fall of dynasties.

Astrology Brings Understanding

People today use astrology to understand their personality better and know what their strengths and weaknesses are. They can use horoscopes to know when there may be upcoming challenges or opportunities. Your response to your environment is determined by personality, and an important factor in your personality is your Zodiac sign and its corresponding quality and element. Therefore, astrology can explain how you will respond in certain situations. This understanding can be used to your advantage or, at the very least, help you to know that it's just the way you are.

For example, someone with the Fixed quality (Taurus, Leo, Scorpio, Aquarius) will often be uncomfortable in times of great change in their life. They could use this knowledge to realize why they are upset and then strive to regain a routine in life. Astrology offers certain psychological insights that are the accumulation of centuries of knowledge. These can be a powerful help in times of uncertainty.

It is important to remember to act decisively when faced with good fortune or looming catastrophe. The planets and stars will not live your life for you, however much they may influence your life. If you do not use the knowledge astrology provides, you have gained nothing.

Using Astrology in Personal Relationships

As it is a matter of great importance to many people, astrology has become highly refined in providing knowledge about significant others. Horoscopes often include advice or predictions involving your lover or crush. You can use your Zodiac sign in dating to have an idea ahead of time how a relationship would work with someone, based on their Zodiac sign and how yours interacts with it.

The relationship between two signs may be likely to work out because of shared interests and personality. Or it could be a cause for conflict, breeding misunderstanding and resentments. However, a good matchup between signs is no guarantee of a successful relationship, nor is a bad matchup a sure omen of a doomed one. Understanding your partner's astrological traits can help you to understand why your partner sees things and reacts to things the way they do. This can lead to more joyful times for both and it can help when working through conflicts. These sign interactions are a general guide to be used with consideration of other factors.

Astrology is helpful when it comes to interacting with your family. Understanding the characteristics of the signs for each of your family members can give insight on their words and deeds. You can learn about why there may be chronic conflict between two family members. You can use it to see an issue from the other point of view, which tends to decrease frustration and hostility. Reading horoscopes to family members can be a fun bonding activity.

For friends, astrology can be used to seek out the friendships most likely to succeed and to know why conflict arises and when that conflict may be irreconcilable, signaling it's time to move on. It can be used to understand the different mindsets of your friends and to know which ones would be best to undertake a project or go on a trip with.

Some signs have very different priorities and knowing and accepting the differences in your friend's motivations can be therapeutic. It can be very discouraging when you are excited about an idea and a friend shoots it down. It may be for a good reason, or it might be just because they have a different sign and mindset. In this case, it's best to share the idea with a friend of a more compatible sign.

ELEMENTS IN ASTROLOGY

The ancient Greeks believed that the world was composed of four elements: fire, earth, air, and water. Everything was a mixture of different amounts of these four elements. These four basic elements are no longer believed to be building blocks of our world, but they remain significant in astrology. In the same way that it was believed objects were composed of the four elements, it is now believed in astrology that the four elements make up our personalities. Each element has certain personality traits, and each sign has a unique mixture of these traits.

"China's Five Elements Philosophy" on chinahighlights.com explains that elements were first associated with zodiac signs in China in the Spring and Autumn period between 770 and 476 BC. Their zodiac signs are different animals, such as pig, rat, and dragon. They had five elements in traditional Chinese astrology: wood, water, earth, fire and metal. Each element was associated with 2 zodiac animals, except for Earth, which was attached to 4. As astrology spread from Asia and developed in Europe, each of the four ancient Greek elements became associated with 3 of the 12 zodiac signs.

Every person has an element, based on what their zodiac sign is.

The Air signs are Aquarius, Libra and Gemini.

The Water signs are Cancer, Pisces and Scorpio.

The Fire signs are Leo, Sagittarius and Aries.

The Earth signs are Capricorn, Virgo and Taurus

Your element affects you in many ways. It indicates certain personality traits that you have and explains how you will handle different situations. Your element is compatible with certain elements, so knowing your element can help you to find friends and lovers who are more likely to get along with you. Your element says a lot about what your strengths and weaknesses are and what kind of person you are. You can use this knowledge to play to your strengths and watch out for your weaknesses.

AIR

People whose sign is attached to the air element are intellectual; logical rather than emotional. They are witty, clever, and outgoing. They are excellent communicators because of their precise thinking. Because they are less reliant on emotion, they can remain calm and calculating in stressful situations.

They are most compatible with air, fire, and earth elements. They can have trouble with people of the water element because of the conflict between their calm logic and water's strong emotion. To bridge this gap, they need to speak the other's language, the language of feelings.

The heavy thinking that comes with the air element can be good or bad. With the Gemini, it causes indecisiveness due to over-analyzing things, but this prevents rash decisions. With the Aquarius, it means thinking about making things better far in the future, but this can cause their head to be in the clouds at times that require practicality. For the Libra, much of the thinking is about other people, but this can be expressed in either empathetic thoughts, or worrying about what other will think of them. Those with the air element would do well to remember that the world is not inside their head and that not everyone thinks as much as they do. However, their powers of intelligence are sure to serve them well in life.

WATER

Those whose sign connects with the water element are adaptable, emotional, and sensitive. They are deep and creative and they have great powers of imagination. They are in tune with the feelings of others and their observant qualities allow them to catch the subtle cues that a person in distress displays. They can be possessive and their knowledge of others emotions can be used for either nurture or manipulation.

The water element is most compatible with water and earth. For those of a water element dealing with people of the fire element, they should wear a thick skin and be ready to not take the fire element's occasional bursts of anger personally. They must remember that fire is impulsive and be patient with these people.

Those who are defined by the water element have strong emotions, and emotions can be powerful and difficult to control. However, emotion is a guiding force in our lives and shows us how to react to different circumstances.

A Cancer is loyal and very emotionally attached to their family, which is why it is good to be closely associated with a Cancer. A Cancer may overreact to perceived insults to their loved ones because they are so protective. The Pisces is friendly and altruistic, and rarely judgmental, but this faith in humanity may lead to them being taken advantage of, which causes many a Pisces to become depressed. Pisces are prone to sadness, but this also gives them an insight into the suffering of others, creating empathy with those in need. The Scorpio is brave and passionately attached to what they believe to be true. This can cause them to fight for something good, or if they are mistaken in their beliefs, to be a powerful force for evil. Their suspicious nature can protect them, but also make them paranoid, and therefore emotionally unstable.

Those with water as their element can overcome any weaknesses associated with emotionality by taking a time-out from the situation. A powerful emotion is like a strong fire, very hot, but quick to burn its fuel and end.

FIRE

Which brings us to the fire element! Those whose signs are attached to the fire element are energetic, impulsive, and enthusiastic. Their liveliness is inspiring and they make great leaders because of their charisma. They can also be very unpredictable and have a temper; they will be forceful when triggered. Adventurous and quick to try new things, people of the fire element are often groundbreakers and innovators. They stick with what their gut tells them and are very decisive.

Fire people are most compatible with air and fire people. When they deal with those of the earth element, they may become irritated with how grounded and practical they are and consider them boring. In this case, a fire person should keep their ego in check and realize that stable people are just as necessary as the impulsive ones.

The energy and charisma of people under the fire element can lead to a wide variety of outcomes. For the Aries, their energy is expressed in their speed and competitiveness. This impatience can lead to greatness, or frustration and anger. They always want to be first, and although they are very organized, their tendency to race through things can trip them up. For the Leo, their charisma leads to unparalleled leadership abilities. But they can also have a large ego and be stubborn and self-centered. Their ability to get their way from others means they might not address these issues, because they won't need to. When it comes to the Sagittarius, part of their charm is their uncompromising honesty. Their trustworthiness attracts people, but it can also drive them away if a Sagittarius says something brutally honest that hurts someone's feelings.

EARTH

The people whose sign is associated with the earth element can truly be described as down-to-earth. They are practical, emotionally stable, and reliable. They are not risk-takers nor are they prone to idealistic ambitions. Instead, they are focused on steadily making improvements in their lives and the lives of those they love. They are materialistic and intent on accumulating money and property.

Earth gets along best with earth and water. To get along with the fire element, earth people shouldn't try to save these impulsive risk-takers from failure, because they won't listen.

The stability and materialism of the earth element has predictable results. The Taurus is reliable yet stubborn and will be conservative in their life choices. They are good at making money, but they can also become greedy because of money's addictive properties. The Virgo does things systematically and never leaves anything undone. They are highly organized but this means they are prone to perfectionism. They can be judgmental of anyone who lacks their attention to detail, which may hurt someone's feelings. The Capricorn is disciplined and self-reliant. They are fond of tradition and value experience over experiment. Their commitment to tradition can lead to stubbornness and they often expect innovations to fail. Their faith in the tried and true can be utterly unshakeable.

ASTROLOGICAL QUALITY

In Astrology, there are 12 signs of the Zodiac. Each of these signs corresponds to one of three qualities: Cardinal, Fixed or Mutable. The qualities are also called quadruplicities because they each describe four of the Zodiac signs. Each quality has certain characteristics that correspond to the position in the season of the zodiac sign. The Zodiac signs that begin each season have the Cardinal quality, or "initiating energy". The Zodiac Signs in the middle of each season have the Fixed quality, or "maintaining energy". Finally, the Zodiac signs at the end of each season have the Mutable quality, or "changing energy".

Your quality says a lot about you and is an important addition to the self-knowledge astrology can provide. A person's quality determines both the inner energy of a person and how they respond to changes in their environment. It explains whether or not they are likely to change their opinions and how likely they are to be a leader or a follower. Knowing your quality can help you play to your strengths and realize what weak points in your energy you need to strengthen. Knowing where one needs improvement can be a path to greatness! Use this knowledge of qualities to achieve greater balance in your life.

Cardinal

At the beginning of each season are the four Zodiac signs with the Cardinal qualities: Aries, Cancer, Libra and Capricorn. These signs usher in the new season and get its momentum started up. Accordingly, people with the Cardinal quality love to start new things; they are innovators and trailblazers. They tend to be ambitious and energetic, eager to start new things. They seem to have endless drive towards accomplishing things, but they often don't finish what they start, because they get so excited about something new that they move on to that!

To go along with their ambition, those with the Cardinal quality can also have a large ego. A big ego is sometimes assumed to be a bad thing, but large egos come with confidence and the self-assuredness of leadership. They want to be the best at everything and work hard to get there. They are creative-types and innovators; trendsetters that the crowd will follow. However, they can be erratic due to their constant shifting of goals, and leaving things undone can cause problems.

Those with the Cardinal quality need to focus on finishing what they start. This may mean delaying a new project they are excited about in order to finish an older one. They can also surround themselves with people of the Fixed quality who will help them reach the finish line in all the races they start. It is very important that Cardinal quality people learn to finish their projects because of how valuable what they begin to create is!

Fixed

In the middle of each season are the four Zodiac signs with the Fixed quality: Leo, Taurus, Aquarius and Scorpio. If we compare those with the Cardinal quality to the hare who takes a nap because he is so far ahead in "The Tortoise and the Hare", we can say that those with the Fixed quality are like the tortoise. They prove that slow and steady wins the race. They have an innate ability to focus and stay committed. They are determined to reach their goals and will be persistent when faced with obstacles. People with the Fixed quality are the ones who get the job done, no matter how difficult or long the journey may be.

Fixed quality people prefer a predictable routine. Once they come to accept an idea or way of thinking, it is very hard or even impossible to get them to change their belief. This can be a strength, such as when they have an important moral belief that those around them have abandoned. It can also be a weakness when they refuse to adapt to new information. Fixed quality people are self-reliant but stubborn.

The best way for Fixed people to overcome their weakness is to open their mind and realize that they do not know everything. The entire universe is not already in their head and they need to be ready to accept new things. There is a Buddhist saying, "You cannot fill a cup that is already full." In this context, this means that when a Fixed person's mind is filled with beliefs that they won't let go of, there's no room to allow new beliefs to come in. Anyone with the Fixed quality should welcome the experience of being proven wrong and take advantage of the opportunity for growth that it offers.

Mutable

At the end of each season are the four Zodiac signs with the Mutable quality: Gemini, Virgo, Sagittarius and Pisces. These signs come at the end of the season, when weather is changing to make way for the new season. That's why the Mutable quality is the quality of change and adaptation. People who are Mutable are quick to follow the crowd and adapt to changes in their environment. This adaptability is extremely important for times of radical change; while those who are stuck in their ways are having problems, the Mutable people will already be back in stride.

Mutable quality people can be shallow, with no deep attachments to any principle, idea or way of life. This can be useful, as some people allow their beliefs to prevent them from seizing an advantage. Being opportunistic and flip-flopping has gotten plenty people ahead in life. However, doing so might get a Mutable person called out on their lack of commitment to ideals which others take very seriously. If they get caught acting different ways with different people, they will lose trust and rumors may spread.

The best way for Mutable people to make up for this weakness is to think for themselves. It's no shame to have other people's thoughts in one's head and be strongly influenced by trends; absolutely none of us are original in everything we think and say. However, the Mutable quality people need to find some time to be on their own and then decide what they think. Then they should take this out into the world and stick with it. No matter what your beliefs are, not everyone will agree with them, and that's okay. Not everyone has to be like you, or even like you!

RULING PLANETS: AQUARIUS

Every Zodiac sign has a ruling planet. The planets are large bodies orbiting the Sun and in astrology they are believed to strongly affect the lives of humans on Earth. The exact scientific definition of "planet" differs from astrology's. For astrology, the moon and the sun are considered planets because they are large bodies in our solar system. The planets alter our destiny and interpreting their movements is one of the main functions of astrology. The position of the ruling planet for your Zodiac sign is a major part of determining your horoscope.

Where do ruling planets come from?

The idea that ruling planets are associated with people born at certain times originated with the Romans. They divided the calendar year into portions associated with heavenly bodies. The Earth was once thought to be the center of the universe. So, when the planets moved backwards and forwards in the sky, or moved faster or slower, they didn't understand that it was because of the Earth's movement. They thought the planets were trying to communicate with humans. The same way observations of the stars predicted the seasons, they thought movements of planets predicted human destiny.

Eventually, Zodiac signs began to be associated with certain months, which led to the ruling planets for months turning into the ruling planets for Zodiac signs. Some signs share a ruling planet with another sign and some signs have two ruling planets, a new one and a classic one. Signs like Aquarius have two ruling planets (Uranus and Saturn) because for ancient astrologers, the furthest planet that they knew of was Saturn. When new planets were discovered, astrologers came to a consensus that some signs would be assigned to the newly discovered planets: Uranus, Neptune and Pluto. Their previous ruling planets are also considered significant, so these signs have two ruling planets.

Uranus, Ruler of Aquarius

The modern ruling planet for Aquarius is Uranus. Uranus represents the revolutionary spirit, because it was discovered at the times of the unprecedented revolutions in France and America. It means going against what is considered normal by society. A person ruled by Uranus has a different mindset than those around them; they do not desire the same things that most do in life. This leads to them taking a different path in life and trying to change the status quo. They want the world around them to reflect the reality within, and the two are very different, so they find they must fight for change. They can be restless: but this drives them to put their energy into improving the world.

Uranus also represents freedom and expanded consciousness. Uranus increases the ability to realize that there is more to life and to see past the controls society puts on us. They are often interested in mysticism or philosophy, seeking to know more about the universe at large and what life is really all about. Those ruled by Uranus are highly intelligent and forward-thinking, always looking to improve the world and make life better for others. Their creativity is a great help in this pursuit. A good way to describe them is "ahead of their time" because their ethics, beliefs, or tendencies often become those of the majority in later generations. For example, Abraham Lincoln was an Aquarius. They seek involvement in humanitarian causes; a rich Aquarius is sure to be a philanthropist.

In moving the world forward, they can be very demanding and judgmental. They see a large gap between the way they think people should act and the way people actually do. This critical attitude can alienate those around them. Someone ruled by Uranus should ease up on their expectations if they are becoming disillusioned, because the average human is set in their ways and will change slowly. If the Aquarius is diligent and patient in leading the way, great events can take place.

Saturn, Ruler of Aquarius

The classic ruling planet for Aquarius is Saturn. Saturn is less influential on Aquarius than Uranus is, but Saturn is still very relevant to those with the Aquarius sign. Saturn rules during the two darkest months of the year. That is why Saturn was once believed to be a bad omen, associated with natural disasters and famines. Now Saturn is seen in a more positive light. It brings challenges that prompt growth. The difficulties that Saturn can bring help us to develop new skills and make important changes; ones we wouldn't have bothered to make if everything was going well.

Those with Saturn as their ruling planet understand their own and other's limitations, which is a skill that many lack. They are responsible and professional and act older than they are; even as children they mature quickly. They tend to have faced a lot of challenges, yet overcoming them has made them prepared for adversity in the future. In fact, those ruled by Saturn may be doing so well in life that others consider them lucky. But it was only their perseverance when they faced strong resistance to success that made them able to excel when their bad luck let up. It's impossible to keep a Saturn ruled person down and as soon as there's nothing trying to push them that way, they are sure to rise.

Saturn represents limitations and that is why those ruled by this planet tend to be very practical. Humans have many limitations, yet our imaginations can run wild, distracting us from the steps we need to take to improve our lives. Saturn allows us to understand what is and is not realistic and possible. Discipline is the strongest point of those Saturn rules; they keep their nose to the grindstone and resist temptation and distraction. You will find the hardest workers among these people; and many of the most successful. Saturn's role is as a teacher and it is hard on its students, which drives them to greatness.

SUN SIGN AQUARIUS

People with the sun sign Aquarius are an interesting and idealistic bunch. Their Element is Air, their quality is Fixed, and their modern ruling planet is Uranus. As I will explain, these details explain many of the characteristics of Aquarians. Rebellious, innovative, intelligent, and unique, people with the sun sign Aquarius are an exciting bunch. They are creative; Aquarians are movers and shakers in this ever-changing world. Like snowflakes, no two Aquarians are alike—not even close.

Traits of Aquarius: Air

An Aquarian believes strongly in ideals and philosophies. This is in accordance with the Air Element, the Element of intellectualism and logic. They passionately fight for causes, sometimes to the point of exhaustion, or even to the point of alienating friends and family by ignoring them to fight for something greater than themselves. They love to learn new things and they spend a lot of time alone, thinking and reading. Aquarians are witty and clever and great with puns.

They are not very emotional in their relationships with others - although they can have deep emotions on the inside, they avoid sharing them. Although they are loving and caring, they enjoy independence and remain slightly detached even from those they are closest to. They may seem distant to loved ones, but they are closer than they appear, because they have affections but don't often express them. They are very truthful, sometimes to the point of hurting people's feelings. This is not their intention; they are just trying to communicate something.

Aquarians are very helpful, even to strangers and they go out of their way to do good and rarely expect a reward. It could be said that they are ideologically generous; they give because they strongly believe that they should, not because of their feelings.

Traits of Aquarius: Fixed

Aquarians have the Fixed Quality, which is the quality of steadiness and stubbornness. Despite this, Aquarians are objective in beliefs and opinions, always seeking to know the facts. They can be persuaded with strong arguments based on reason, unlike most people in the three other sun signs with the Fixed Quality.

However, once they come to believe something, no small thing can detach them from their belief. They love their ideas and will stick up for them; they can debate with considerable skill. Because Aquarians are so smart, they might reject conflicting opinions because they think they know better, but will still change their minds if the truth is right in front of their face.

Traits of Aquarius: Uranus

An Aquarian is a visionary, a rebel at times, and a great force for change in the world, because they are ruled by Uranus, the revolutionary planet. They can be described as eccentric and are proud of it. They cherish their quirks and the ability to express their innermost self in any way they choose. They enjoy research and new ideas and love to be on the cutting edge, whether it be in science or society. Aquarians are adventurous and love new places and experiences.

Aquarius is a humanitarian sign and these people are always pushing for improvement in society. They can be radicals when they see that change will not come within the system, but are also quite practical and patient in that they know when changes must come slowly. They have excellent intuition; they don't "go with their gut", but they do go with their brain and act decisively when they have good ideas.

Aquarian Likes

Aquarians are very fond of acting and they are natural mimics; they love watching good plays. They enjoy being creative and artistic and they love freedom. They like to daydream and make grand plans. They like unusual things and people. Aquarians love their private time and can enjoy themselves when they're alone.

They are very fond of optimism and positive attitudes. They like change, surprises, and new experiences. Aquarians love to travel: the further away the better. Trying new things is a must for Aquarius. They like overseeing ambitious projects. Success in business is very fulfilling for them. They're very fond of getting recognition for their accomplishments.

They like loyalty in friends and partners and will return it; and they like making new friends. They enjoy technology and cool new gadgets. Aquarians like knowing all the facts, being the smartest person in the room and learning new things. They especially like learning secrets about others; they love any insider knowledge that few have access to.

Aquarian Dislikes

Aquarians dislike outdated or very traditional ways of doing things. They don't like being censored or told that their viewpoint isn't valid. They don't like narrow-minded people. They hate intolerance and bigotry and will have trouble controlling their anger when someone flexes their racism. They don't like conflict and arguments; they prefer cool-headed debates. They don't like changing their minds and must be faced with irrefutable evidence if they are going to.

Aquarians can't stand to be bored or stuck in a rut. If someone has too many expectations of them or takes away from the Aquarian's personal time, they will be resented. This means they don't like possessive people, or anyone clingy. Too many rules are unbearable for an Aquarian and they can be uncomfortable in a business environment that doesn't encourage creativity. They don't like constantly being given orders from a boss if they have no input.

They don't like bragging or egotistical people, and Aquarians are angry when those people are being rewarded for their selfishness. Anyone rude rubs an Aquarian wrong. They don't like when people don't keep their promises, or don't even remember making them.

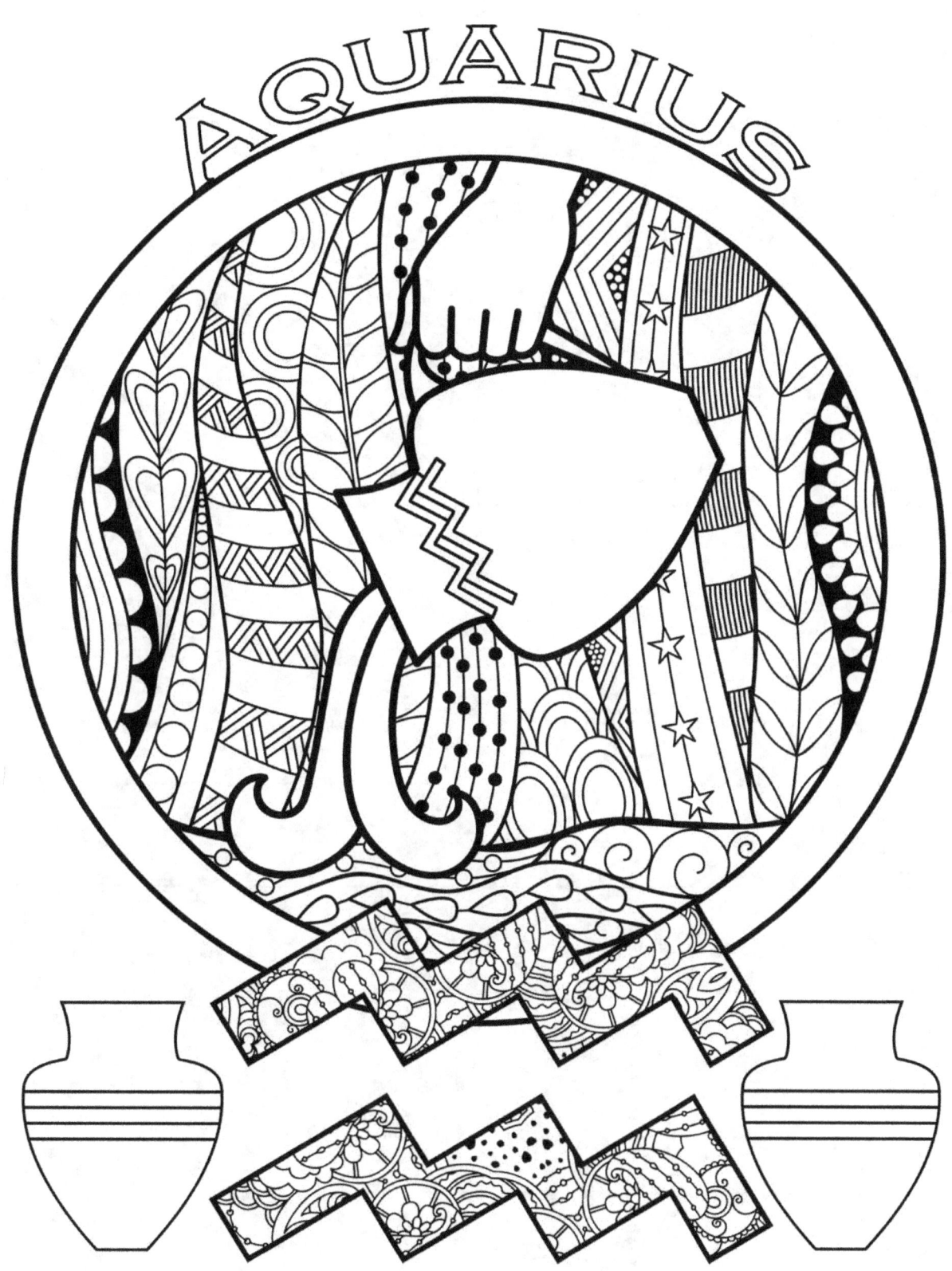

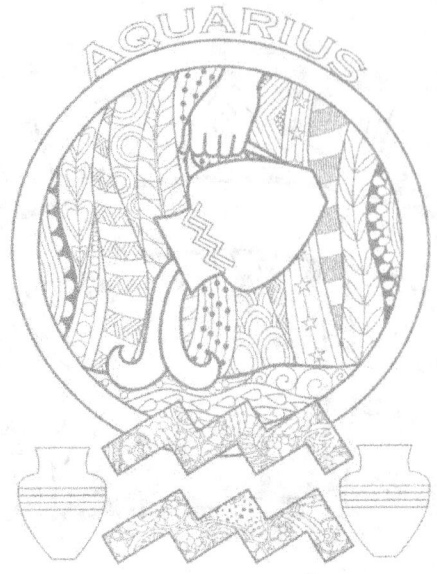

Often eccentric, Aquarians enjoy the bizarre.

_____

_____

_____

_____

_____

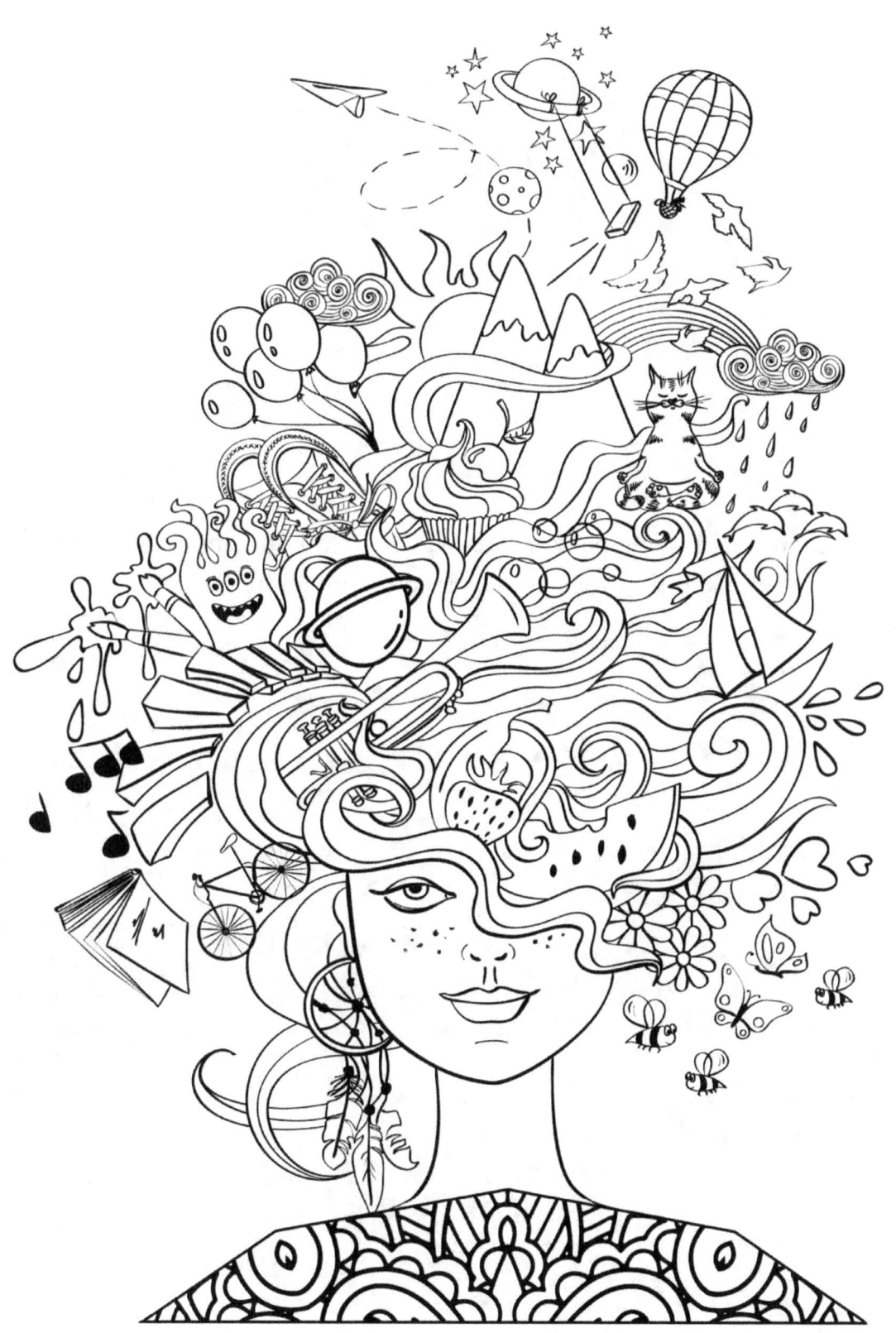

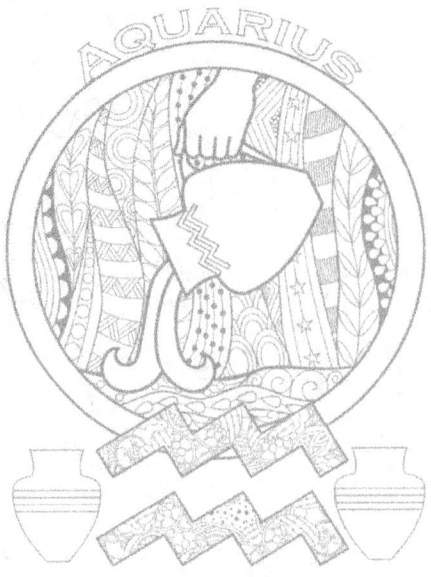

With Uranus as a ruling planet Aquarians seek to know more about what life is really all about and find yoga and/or meditation helpful.

_____

_____

_____

_____

_____

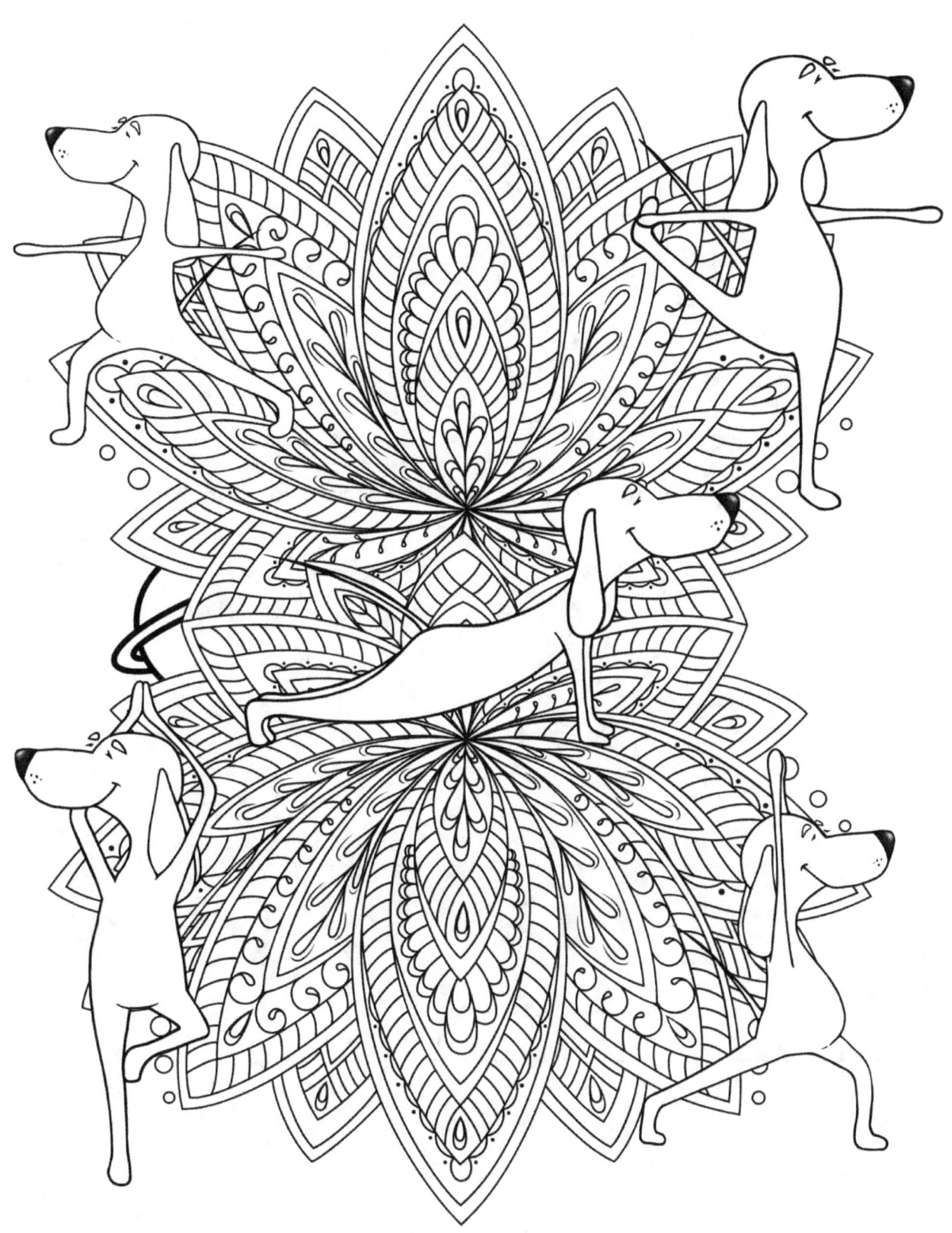

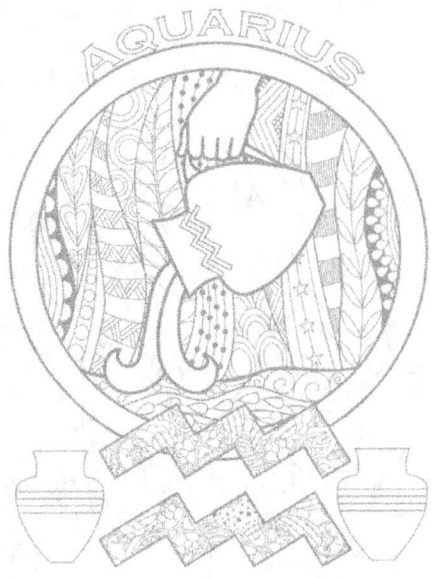

Aquarius people enjoy marathons and are especially fond of charity races.

_____

_____

_____

_____

_____

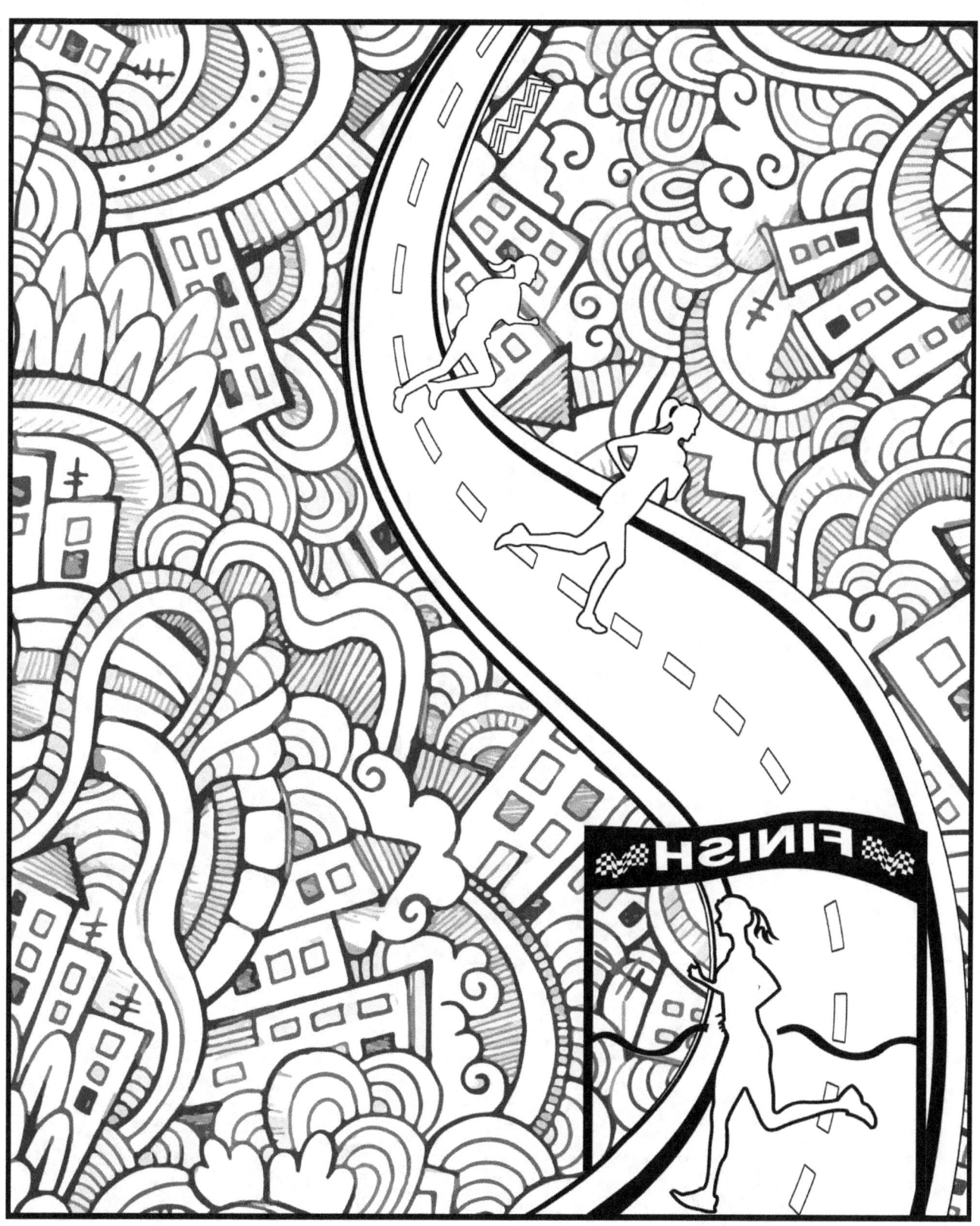

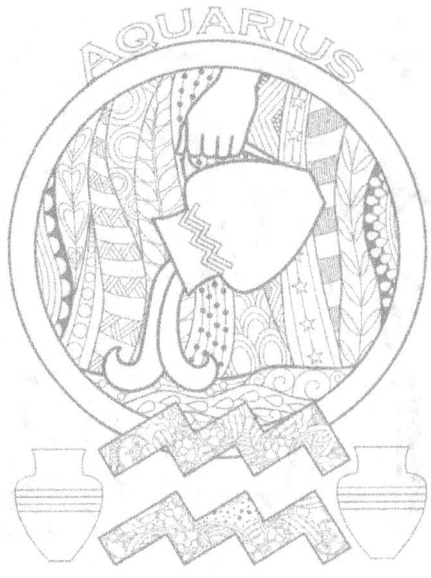

Aquarians like to have time alone, thinking and reading.

_____

_____

_____

_____

_____

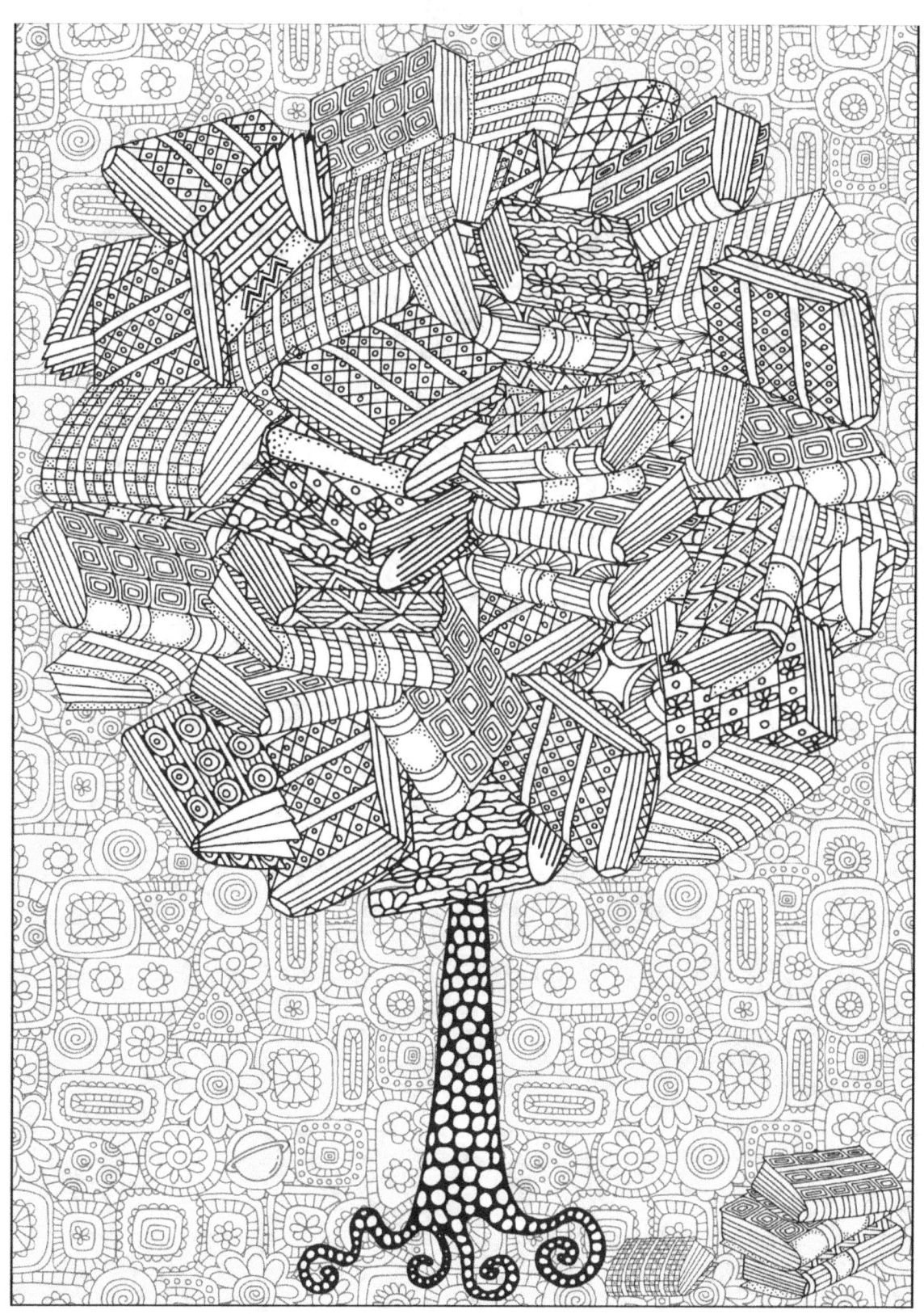

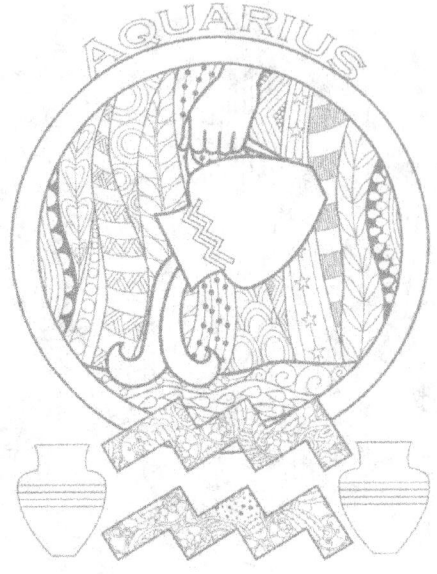

Creative as they are, Aquarians enjoy music.

_____

_____

_____

_____

_____

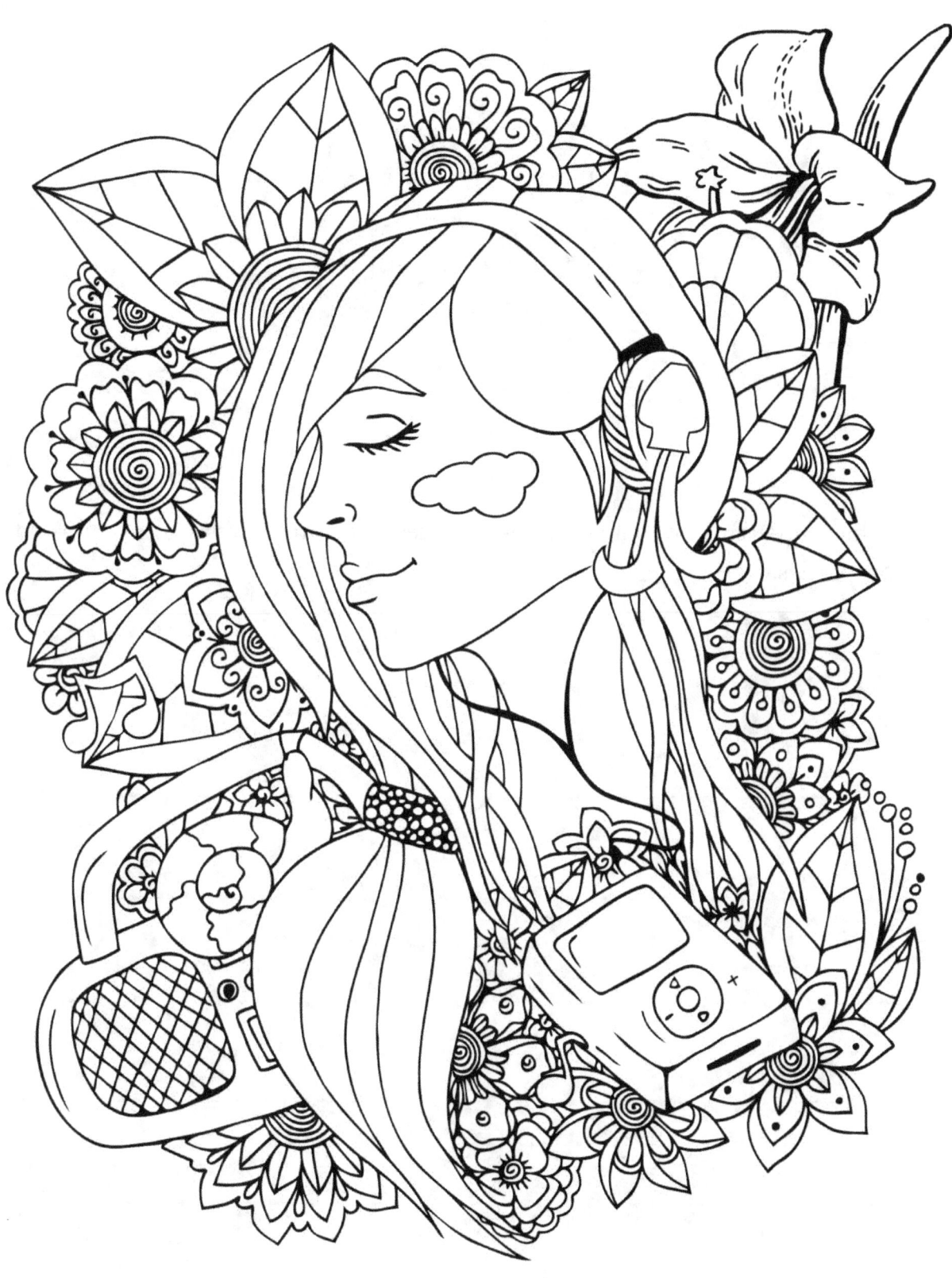

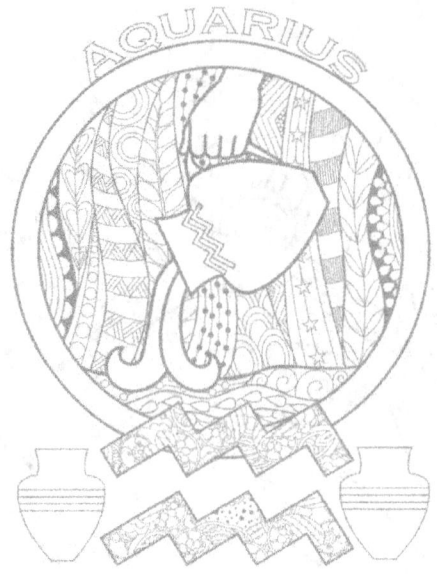

While Aquarians love cities and busy places, they prefer quirky, one-of-a-kind properties.

_____

_____

_____

_____

_____

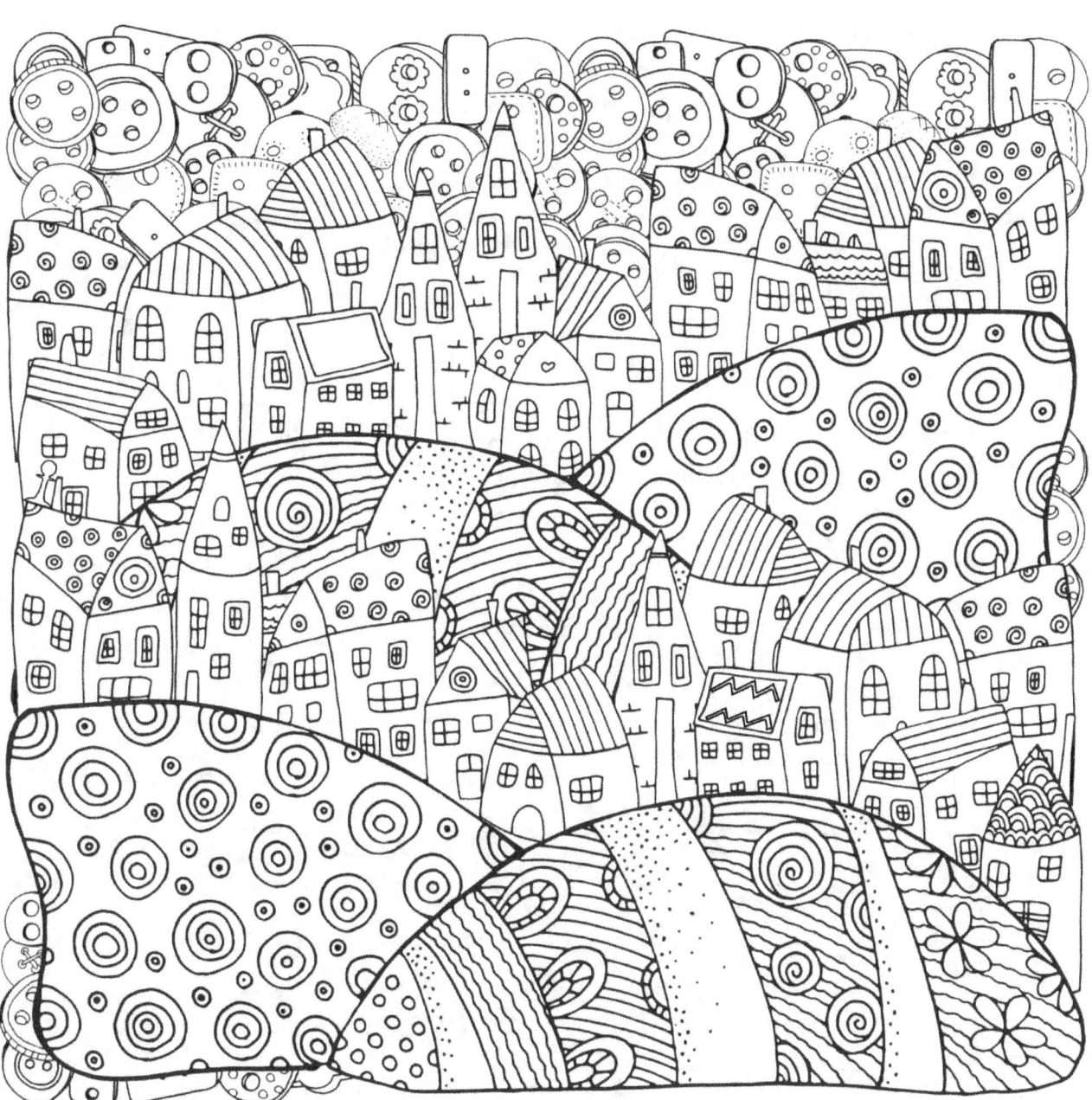

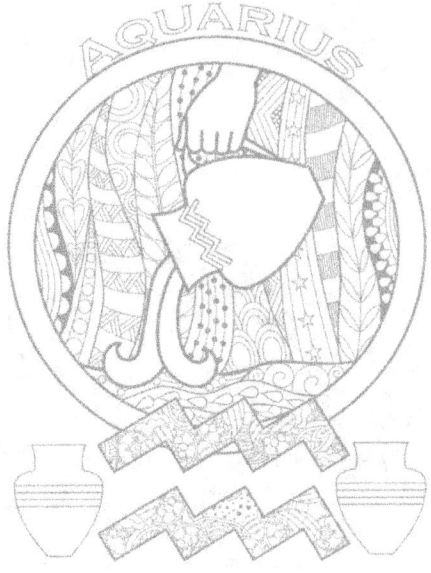

Aquarians are very unconventional and always full of excitement. Being an air sign they enjoy activities like ballooning.

_____

_____

_____

_____

_____

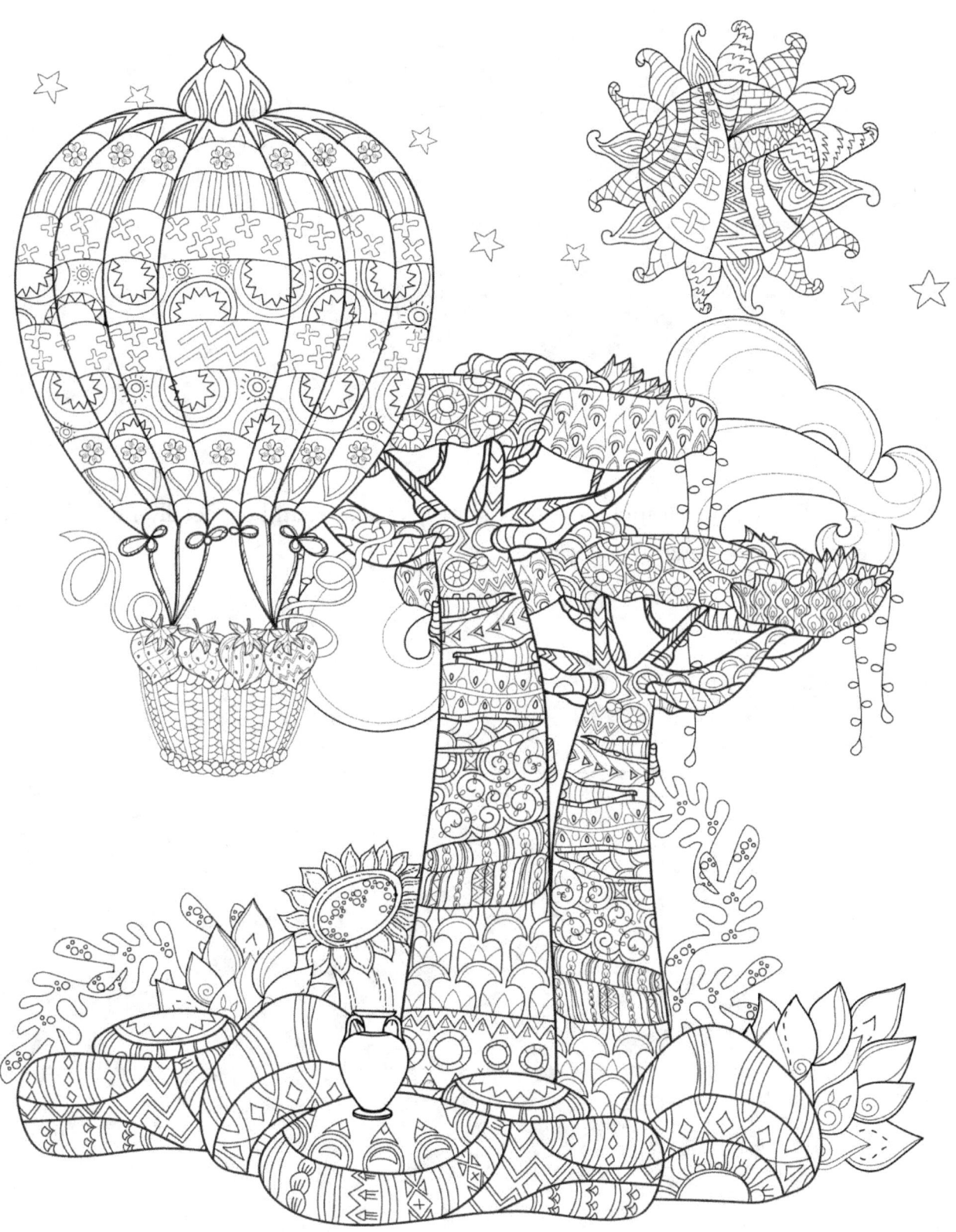

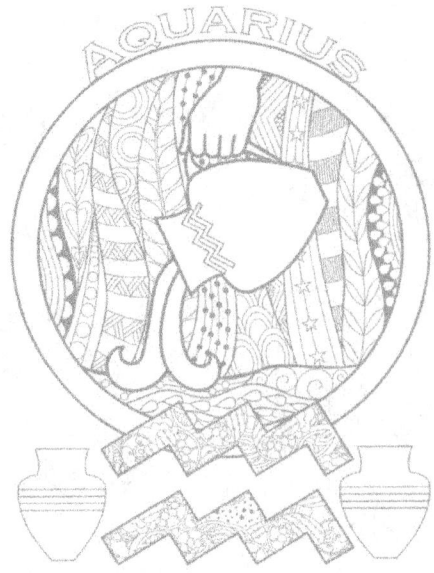

Casual footwear that includes sport shoes, sneakers, and especially flip flops are the favorite of Aquarius people.

_____

_____

_____

_____

_____

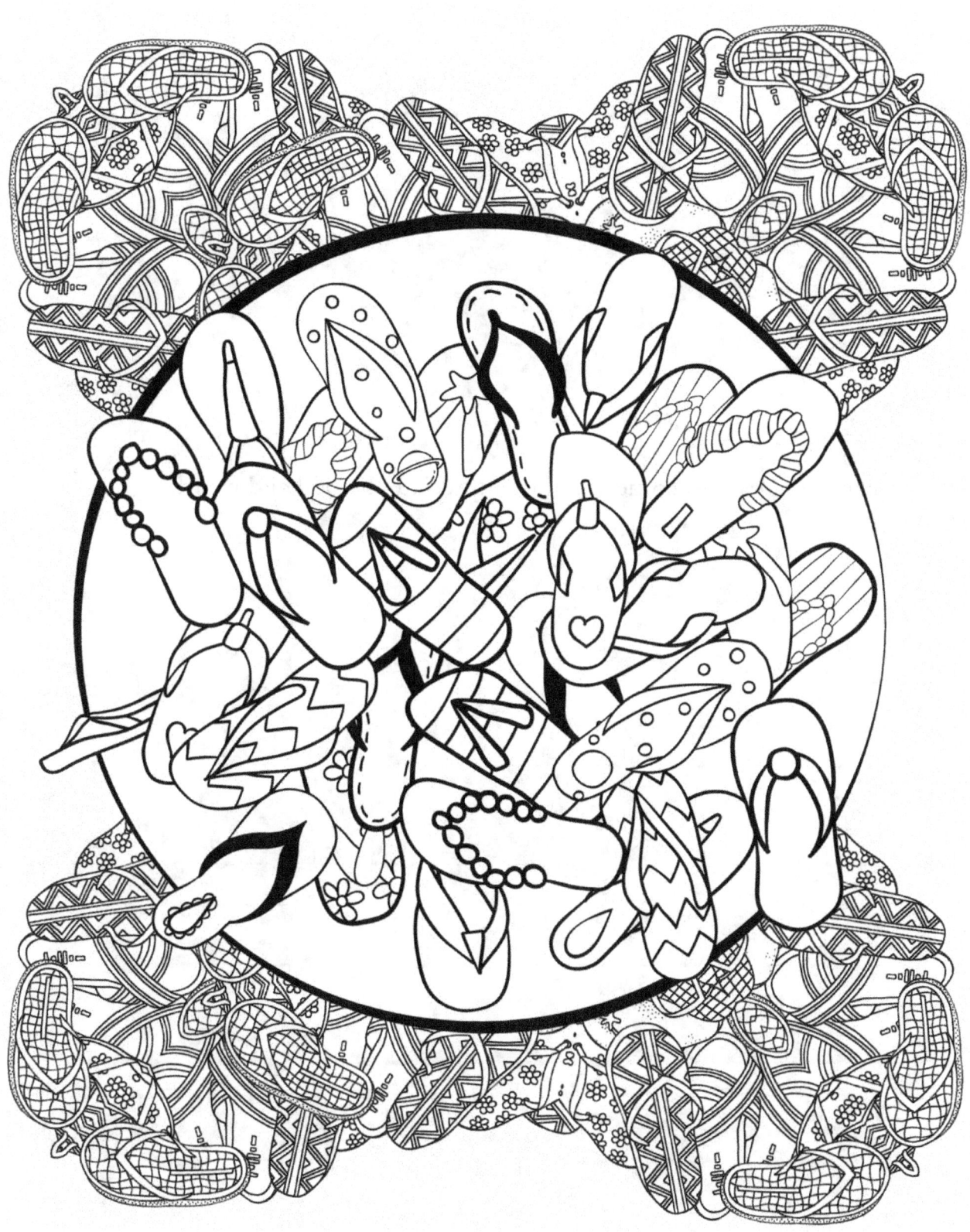

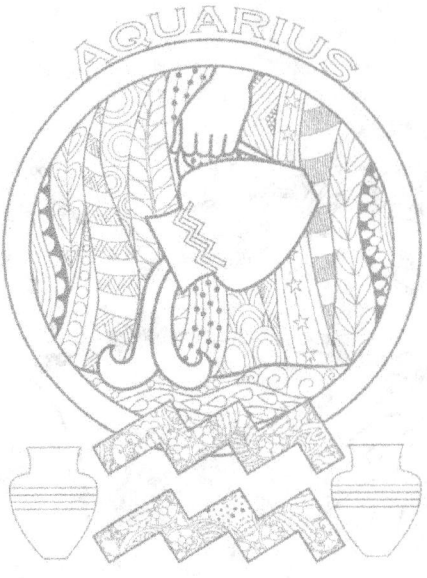

Every Aquarian is unique and they appreciate the odd and weird.

_____

_____

_____

_____

_____

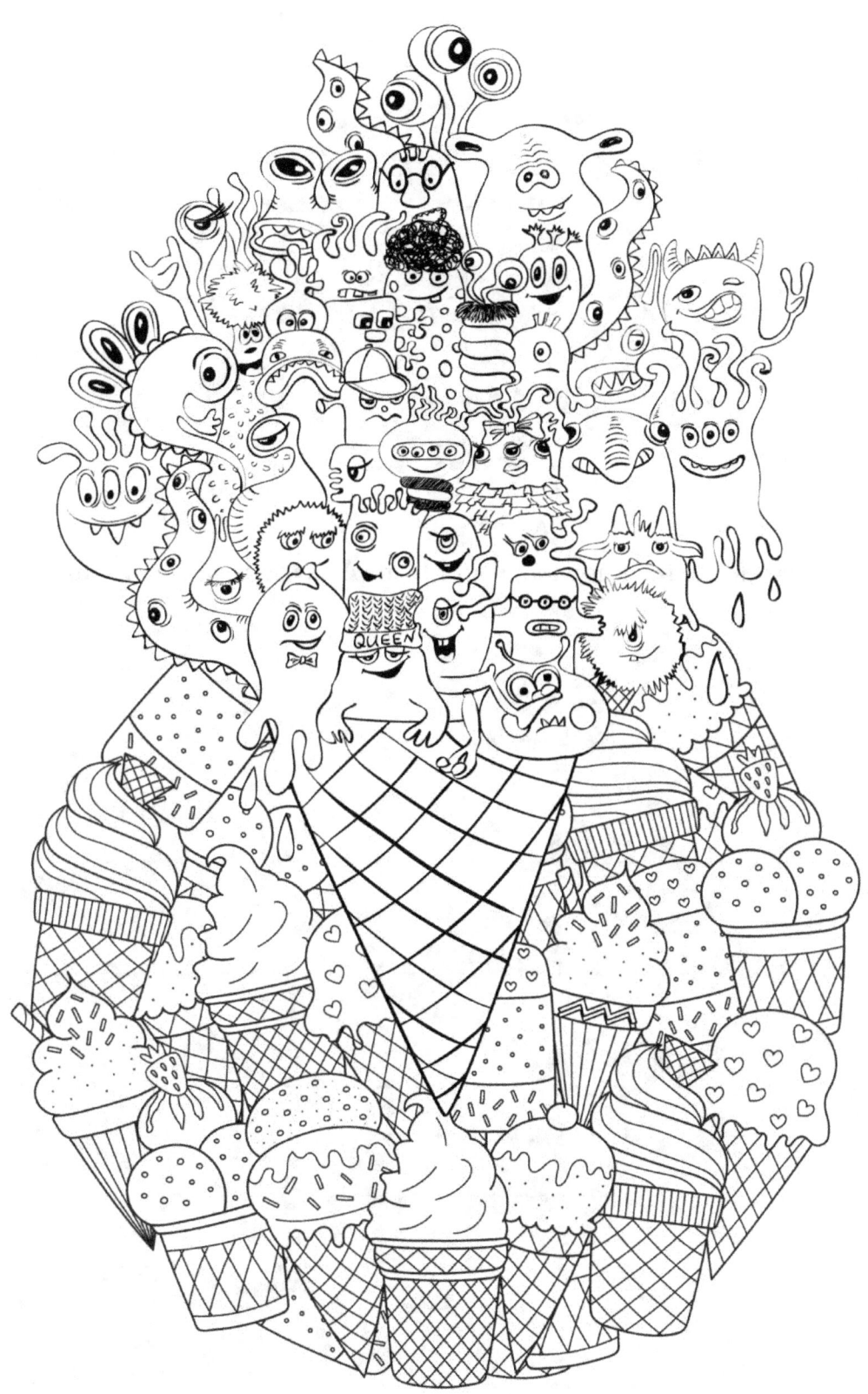

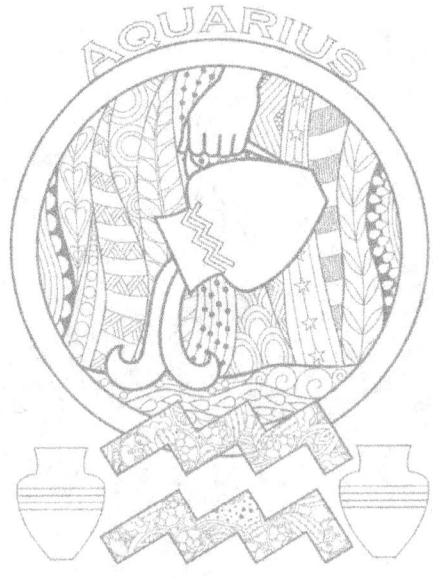

With their desire for knowledge and truth Aquarians have an affinity for astronomy.

_____

_____

_____

_____

_____

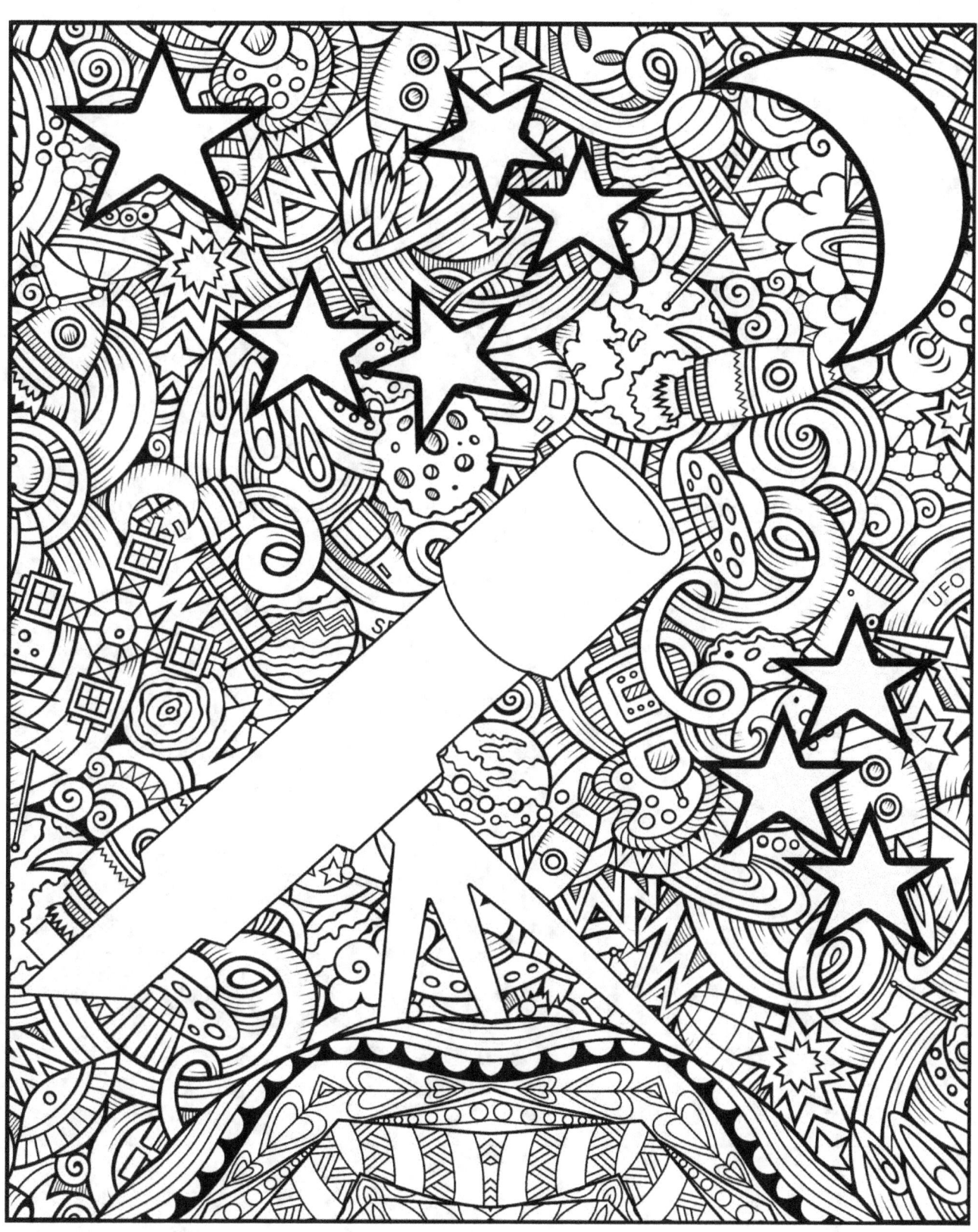

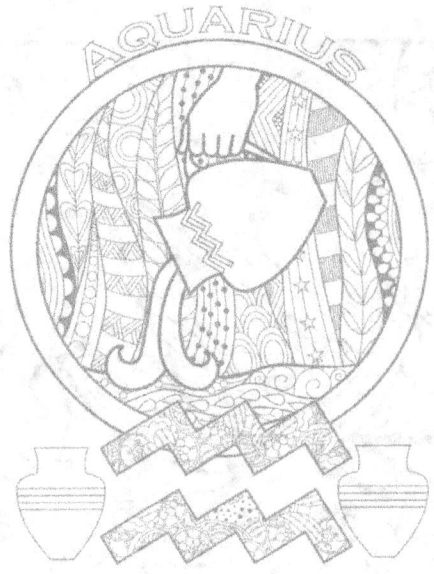

Since Uranus represents expanded consciousness many Aquarians enjoy meditation.

_____

_____

_____

_____

_____

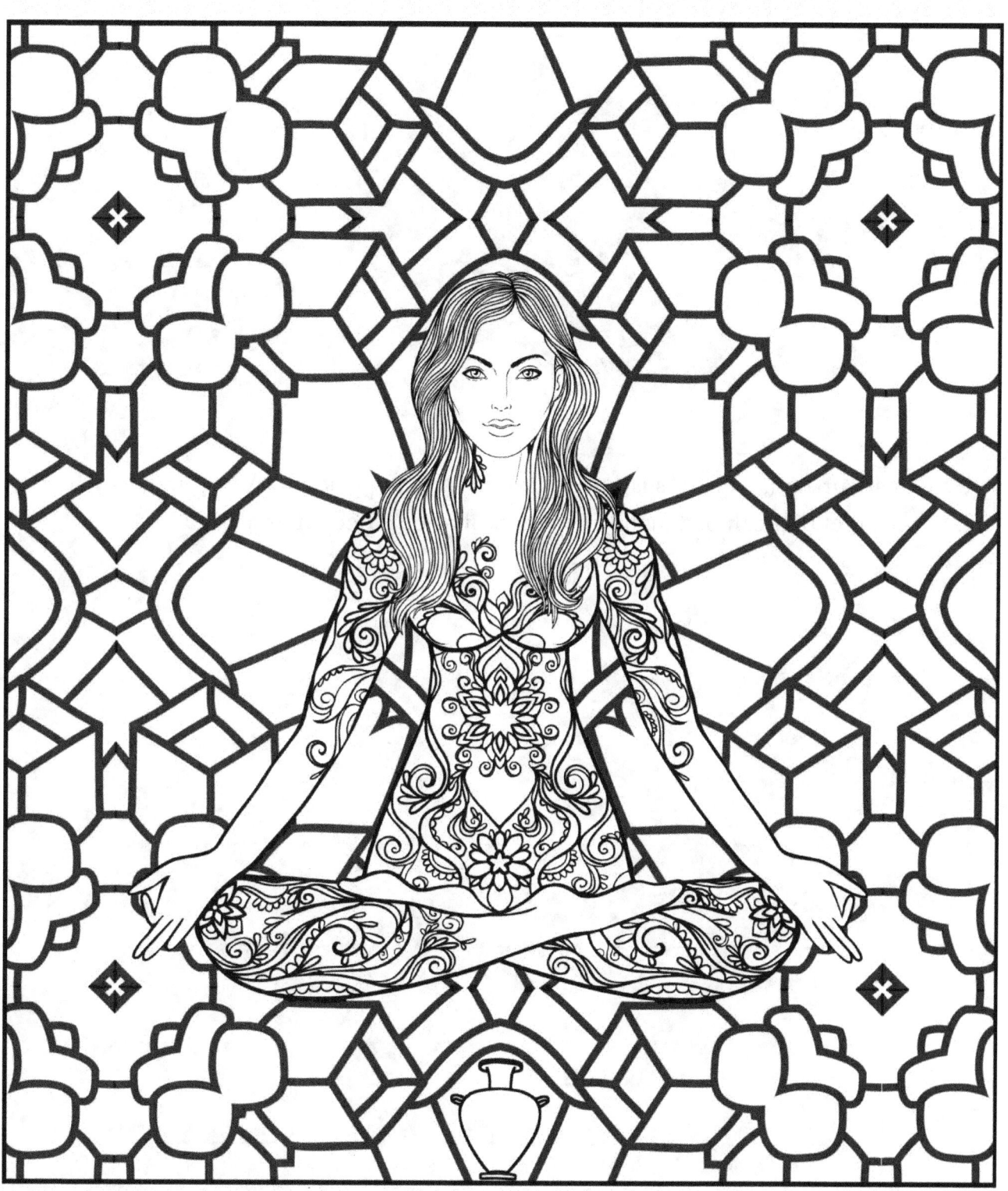

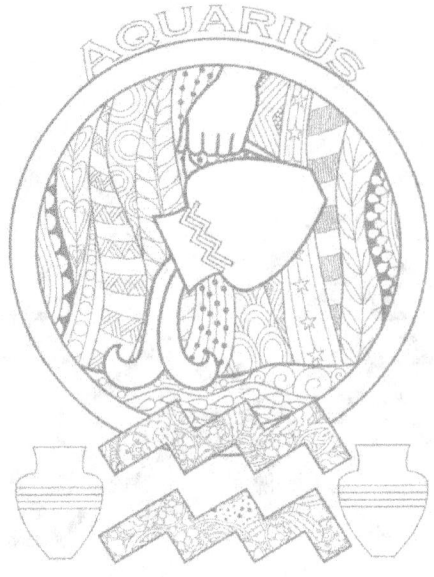

As an air sign, Aquarius is ruled by speed and a quick wit. A bright colored cockatiel that can be taught to speak would be a delight as a pet.

_____

_____

_____

_____

_____

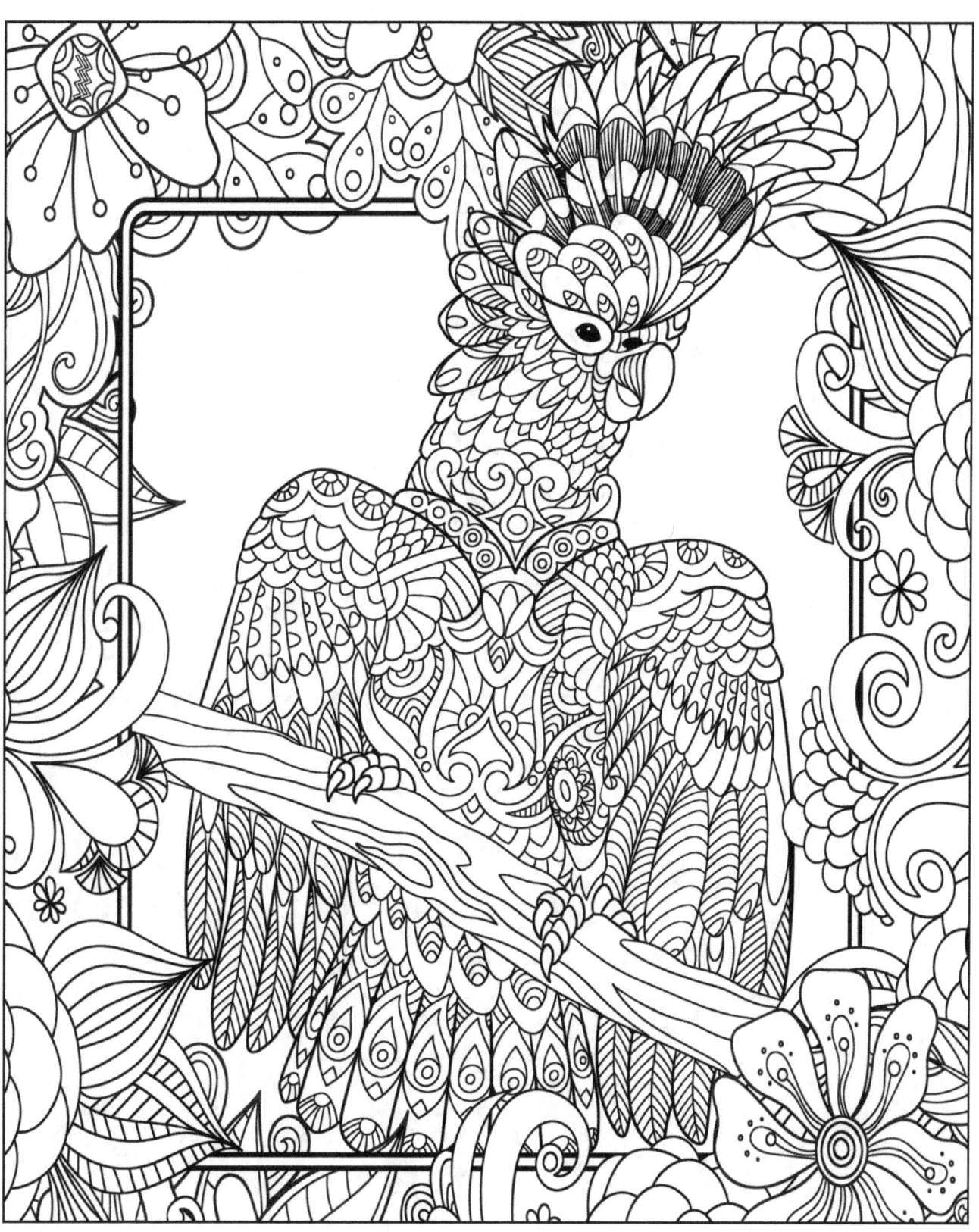

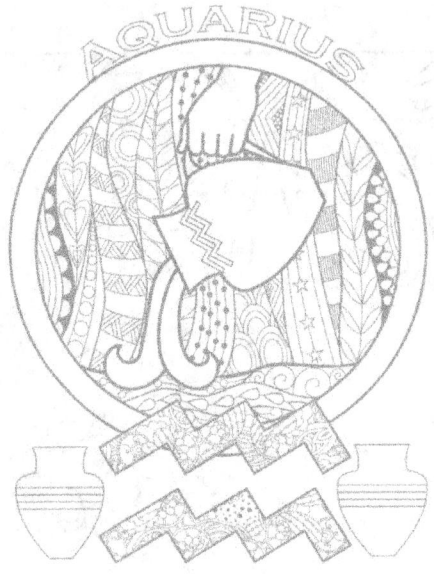

Urbanites that they are, Aquarians value community.

_____

_____

_____

_____

_____

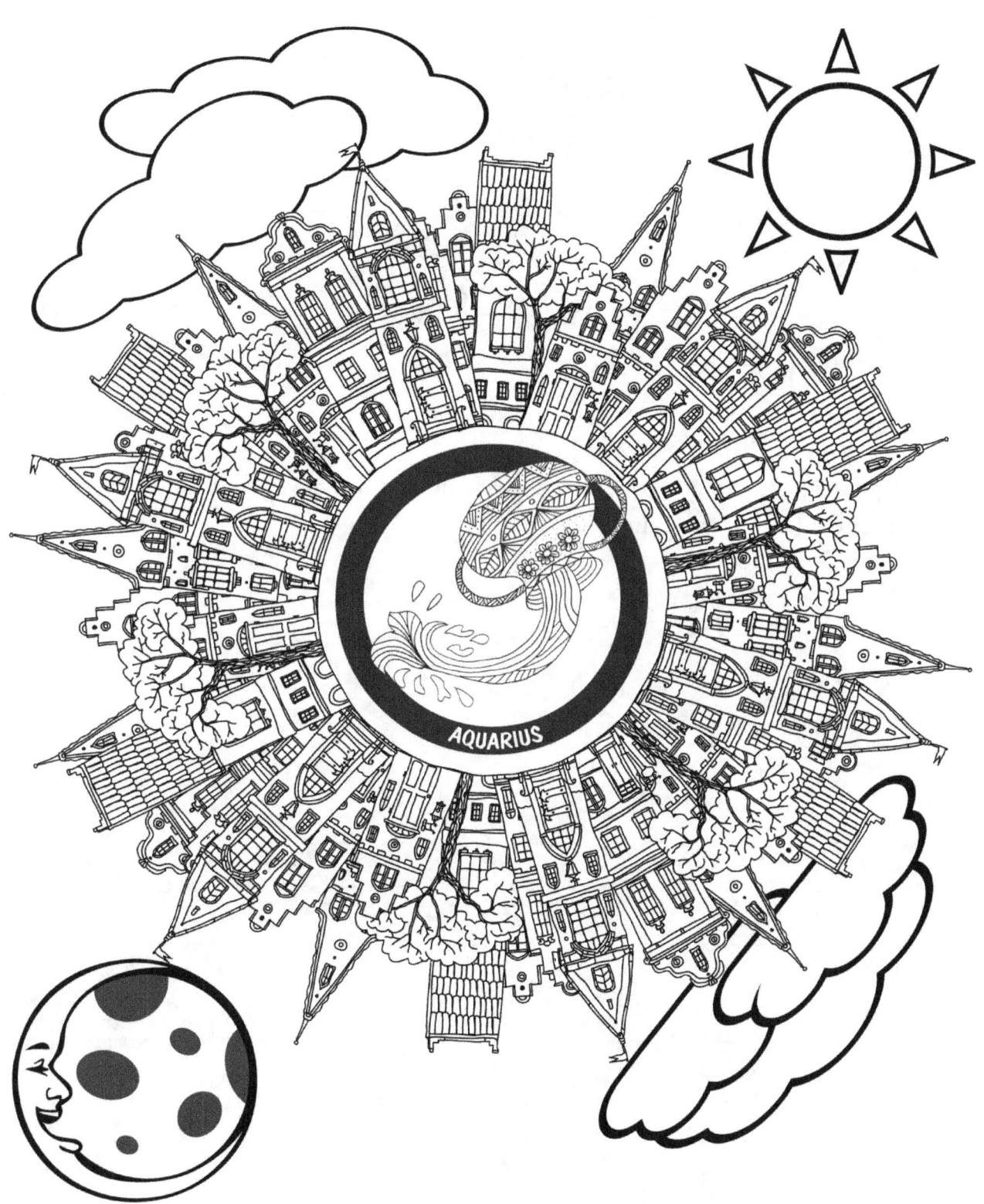

AQUARIUS

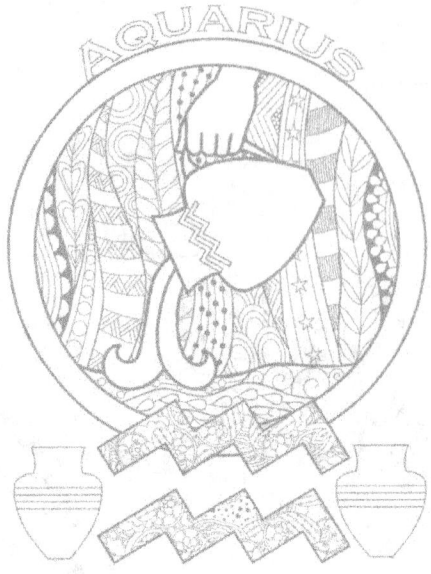

Aquarians fall into two principle types: one shy, sensitive, gentle and patient; the other exuberant, lively and exhibitionist.

_____

_____

_____

_____

_____

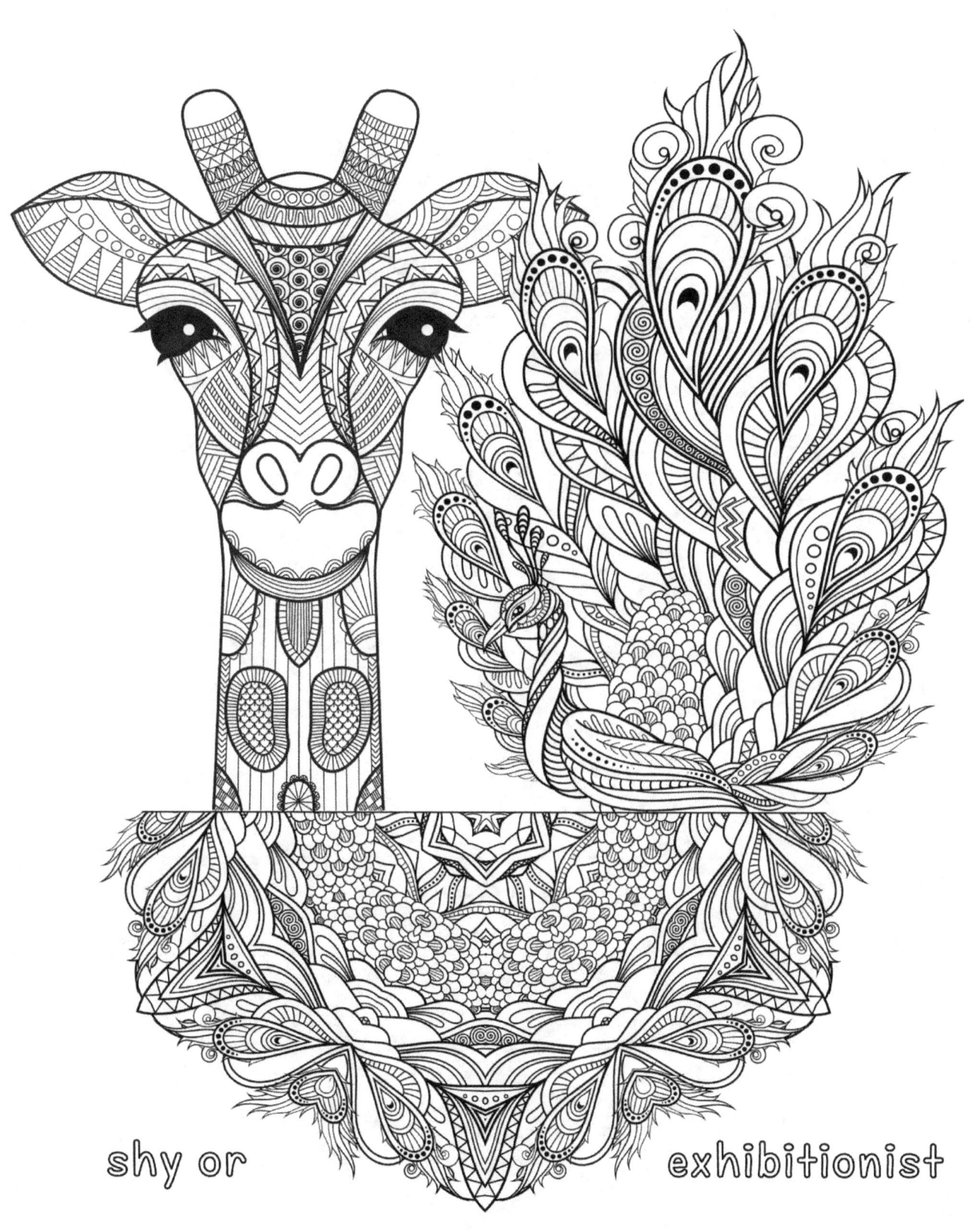

shy or   exhibitionist

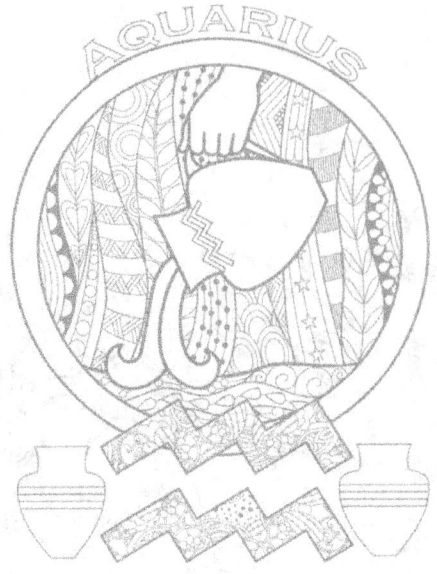

Aquarians like to daydream and make grand plans.

_____

_____

_____

_____

_____

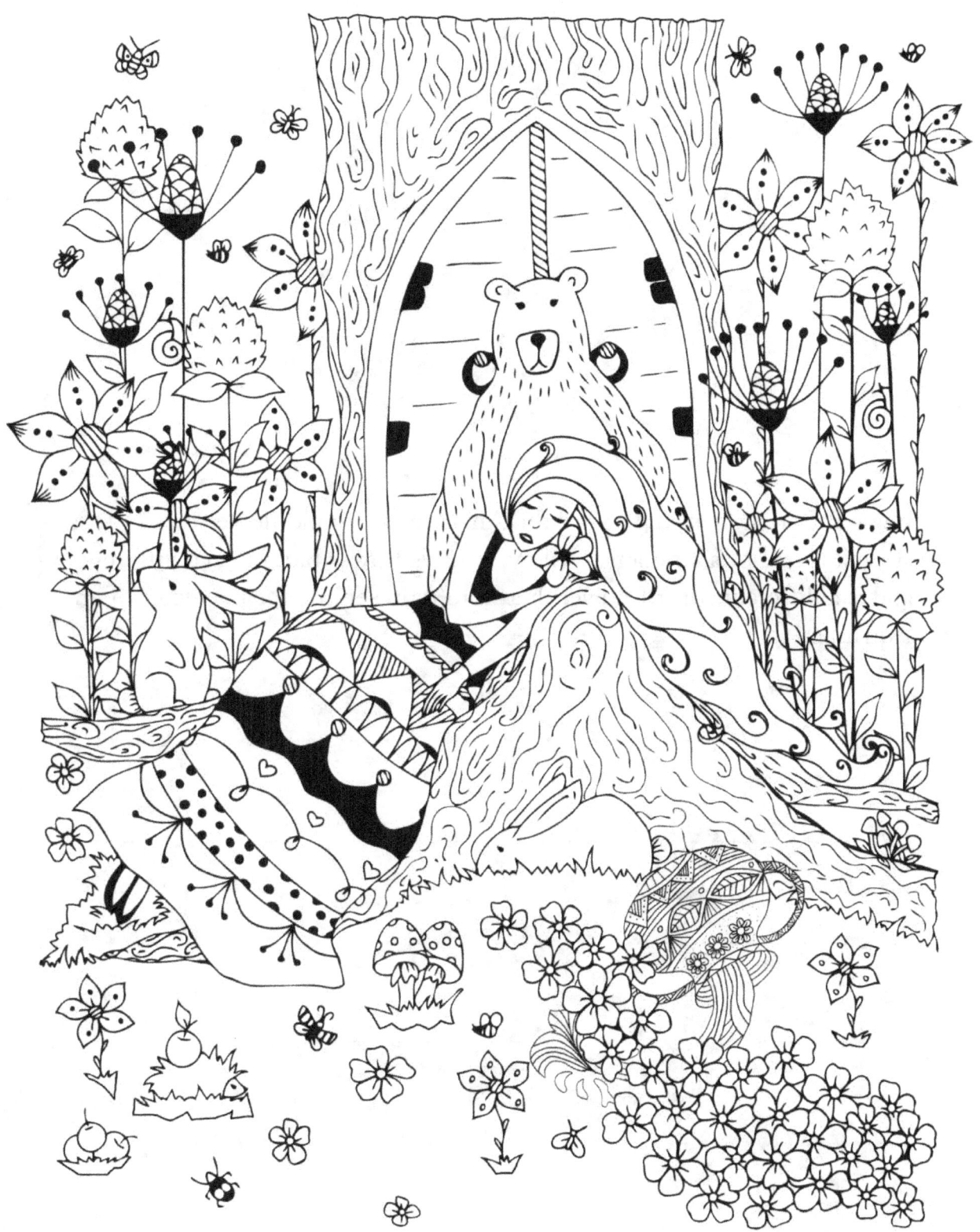

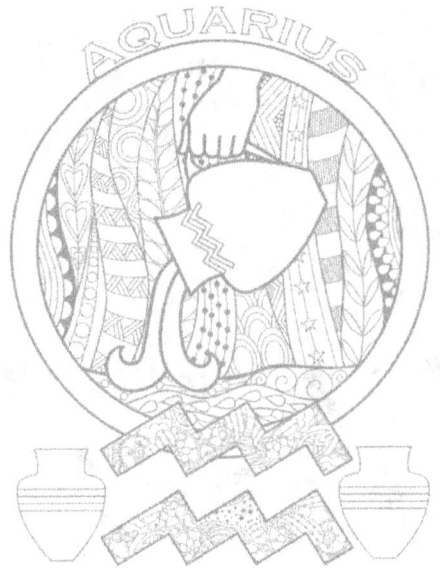

Being different from the crowd the Amaryllis is a good flower for Aquarians since it is one of a kind among flowers. This flower blooms in a different season and is a different sort of flower therefore representing the character of an Aquarian.

_____

_____

_____

_____

_____

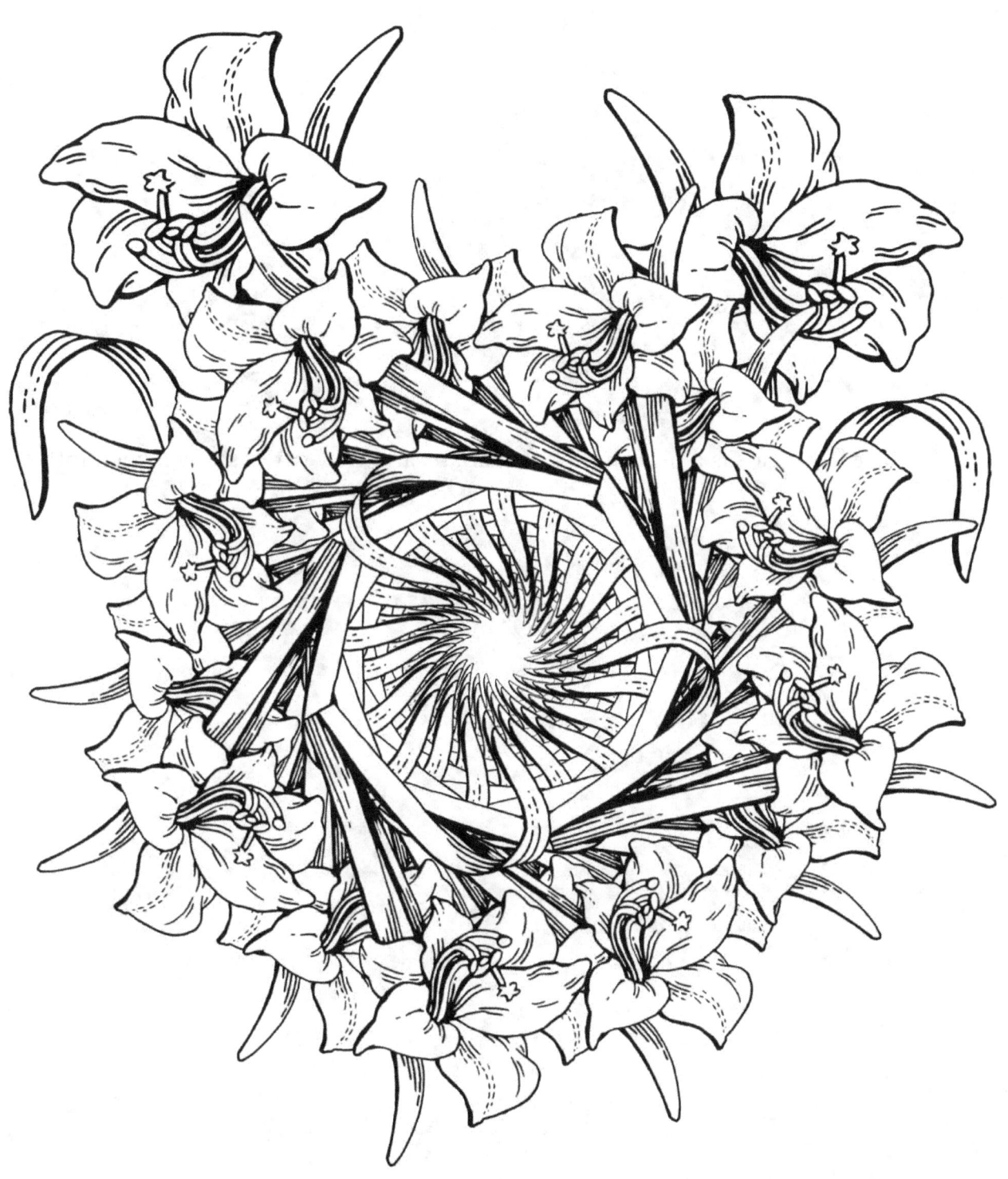

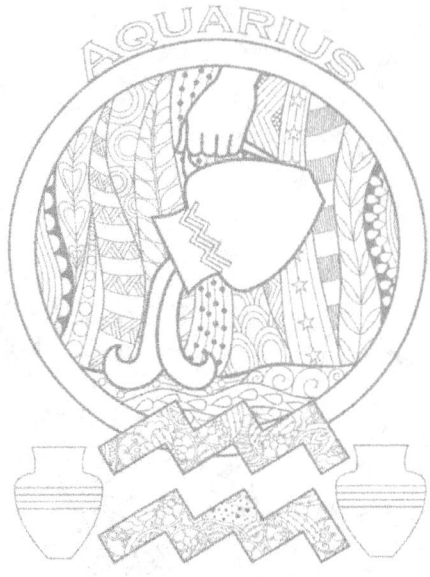

Music of all kinds is a pleasure for Aquarians and they often show a keen interest in dancing.

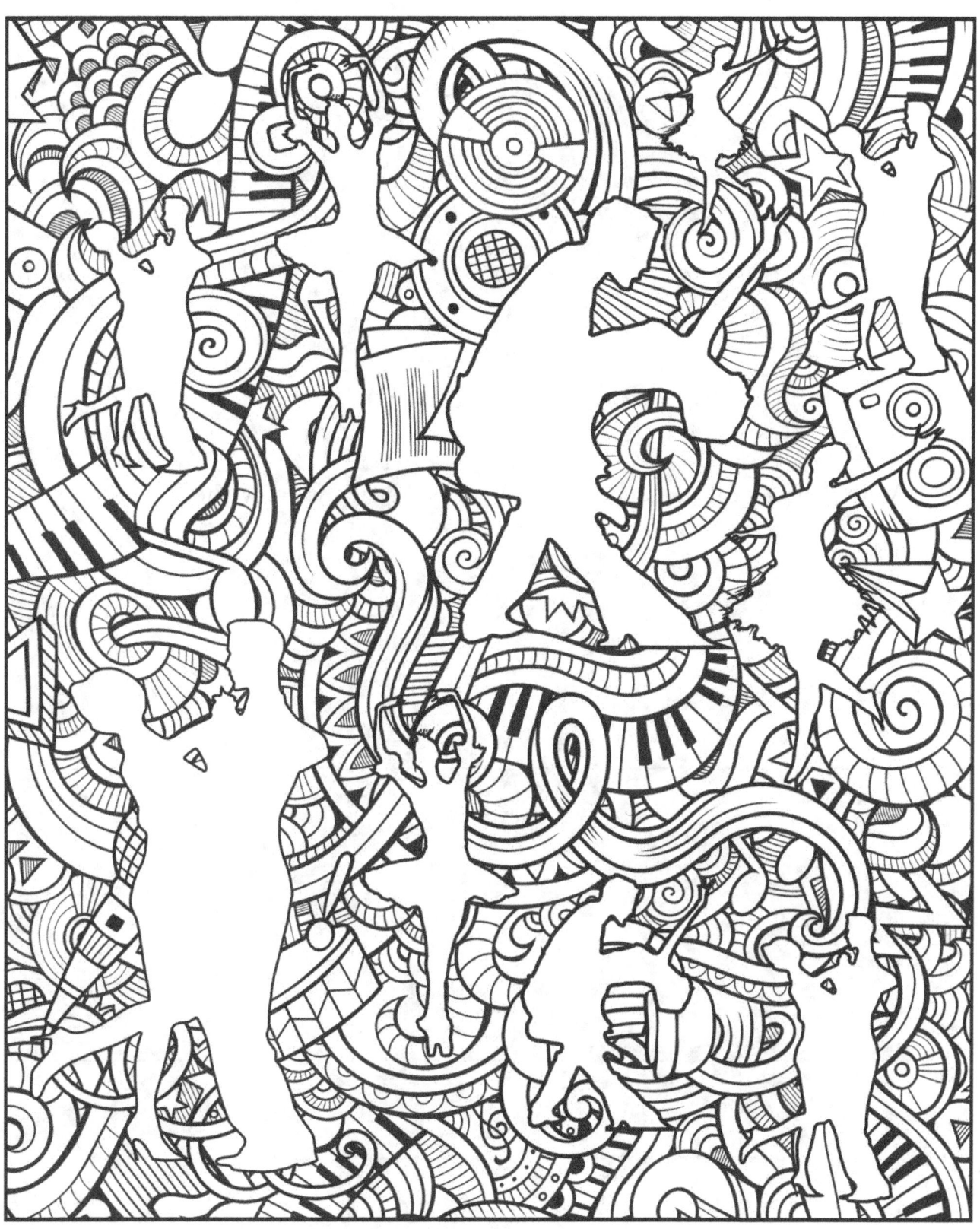

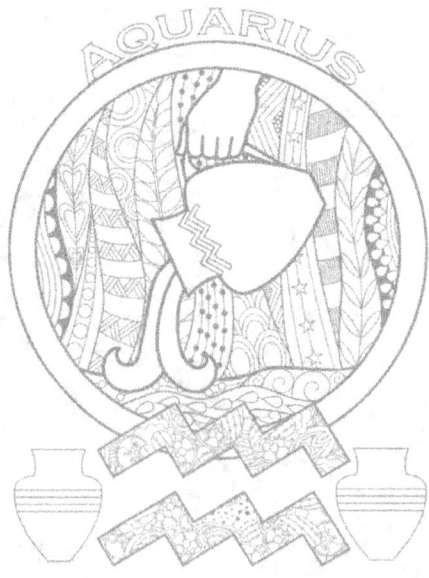

With their logical and strategic mind, many Aquarians enjoy chess.

_____

_____

_____

_____

_____

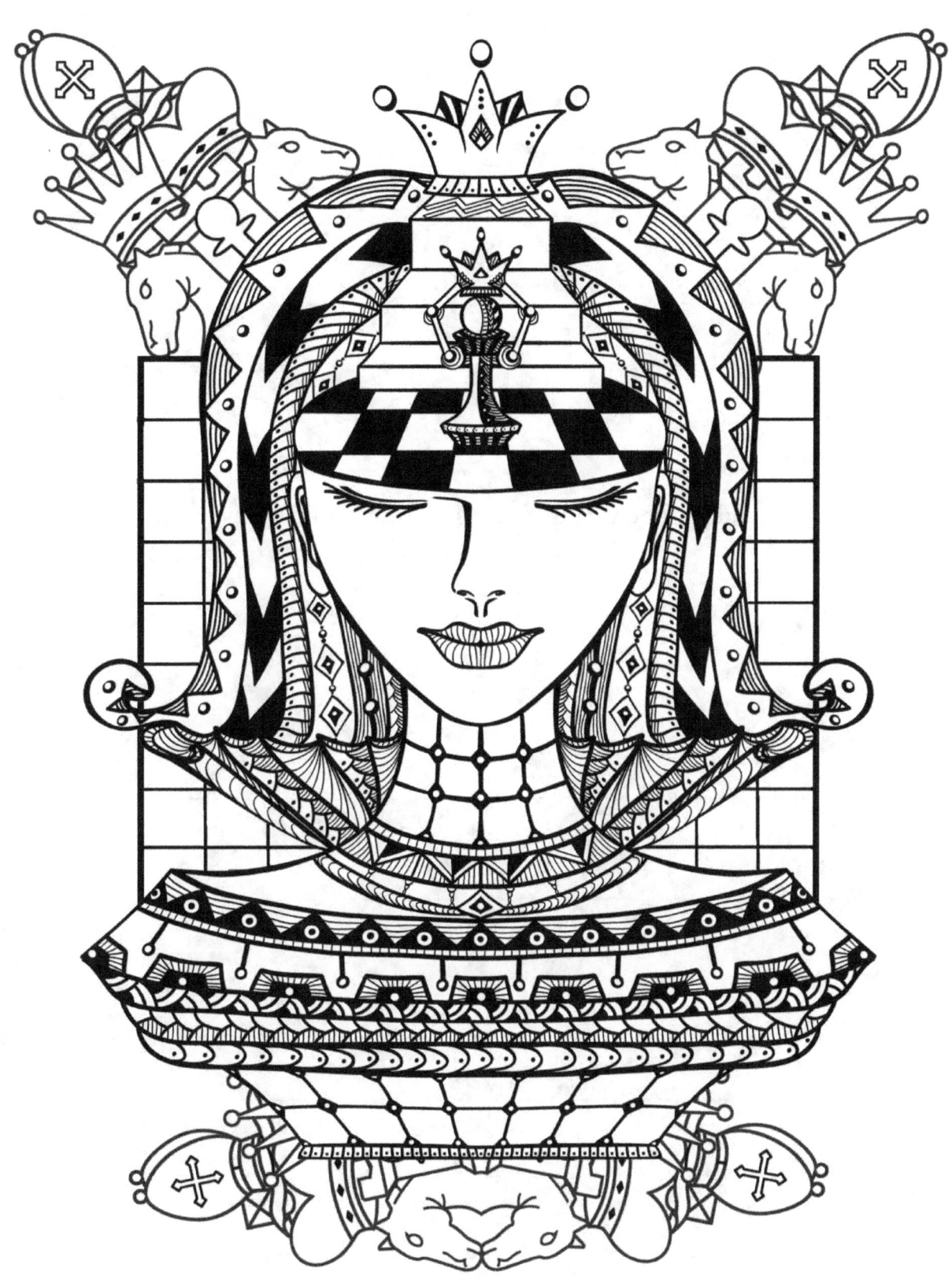

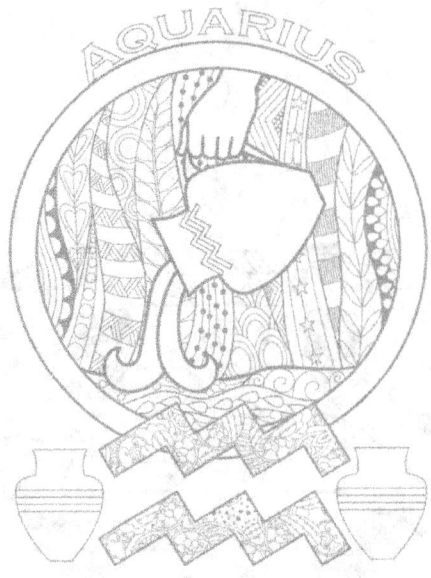

Technology and cool new gadgets are something Aquarians enjoy.

_____

_____

_____

_____

_____

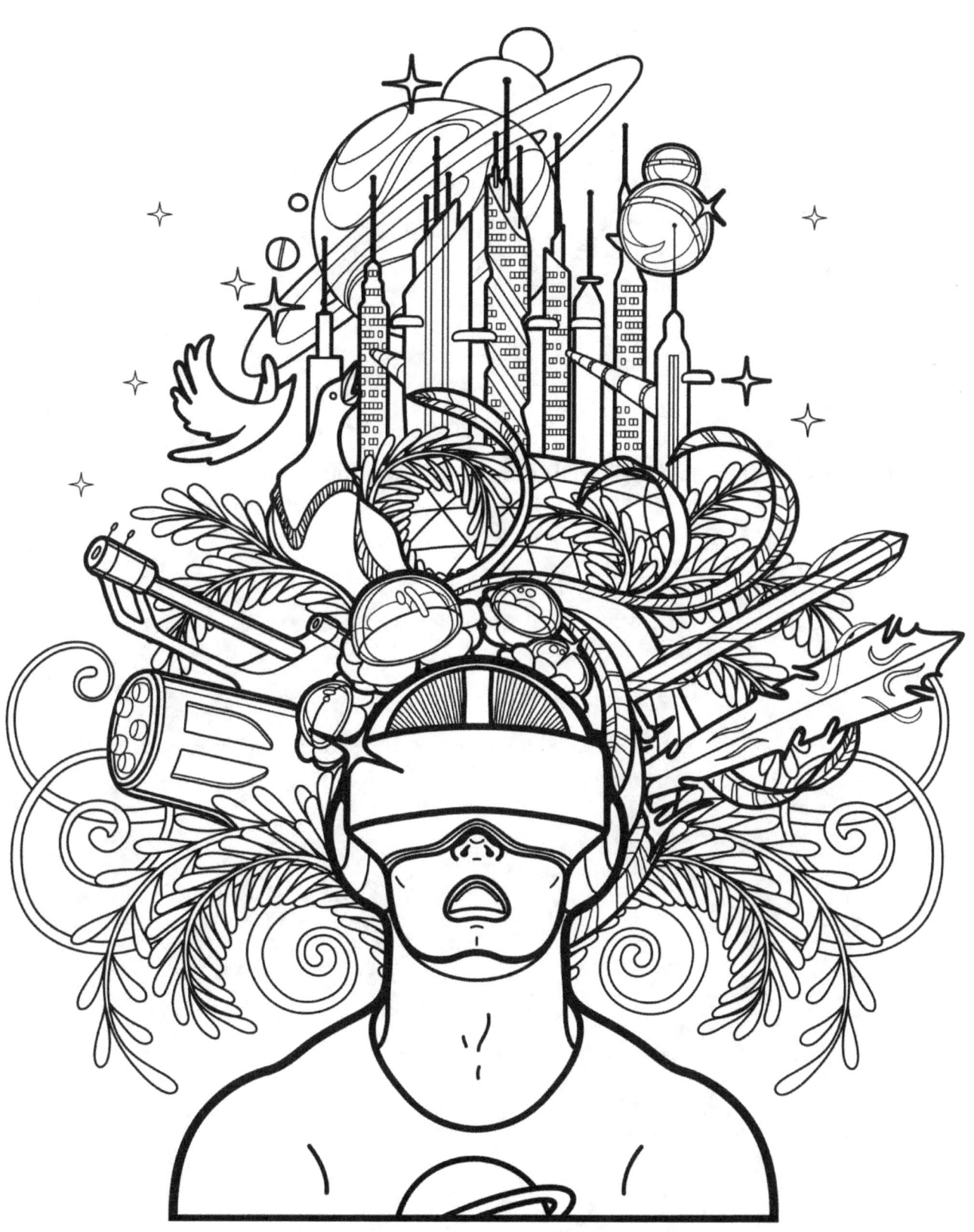

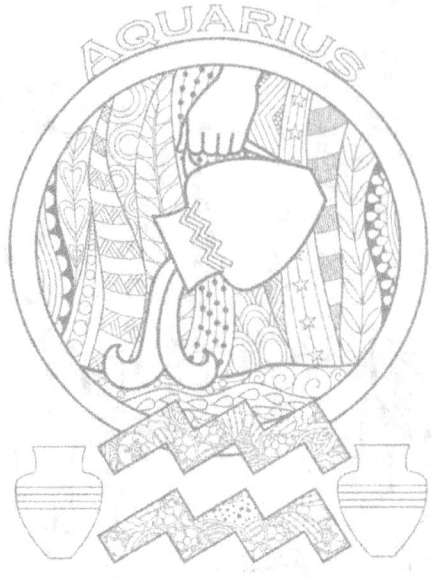

Orchids are flowers considered to be under Aquarius' rule.

_____

_____

_____

_____

_____

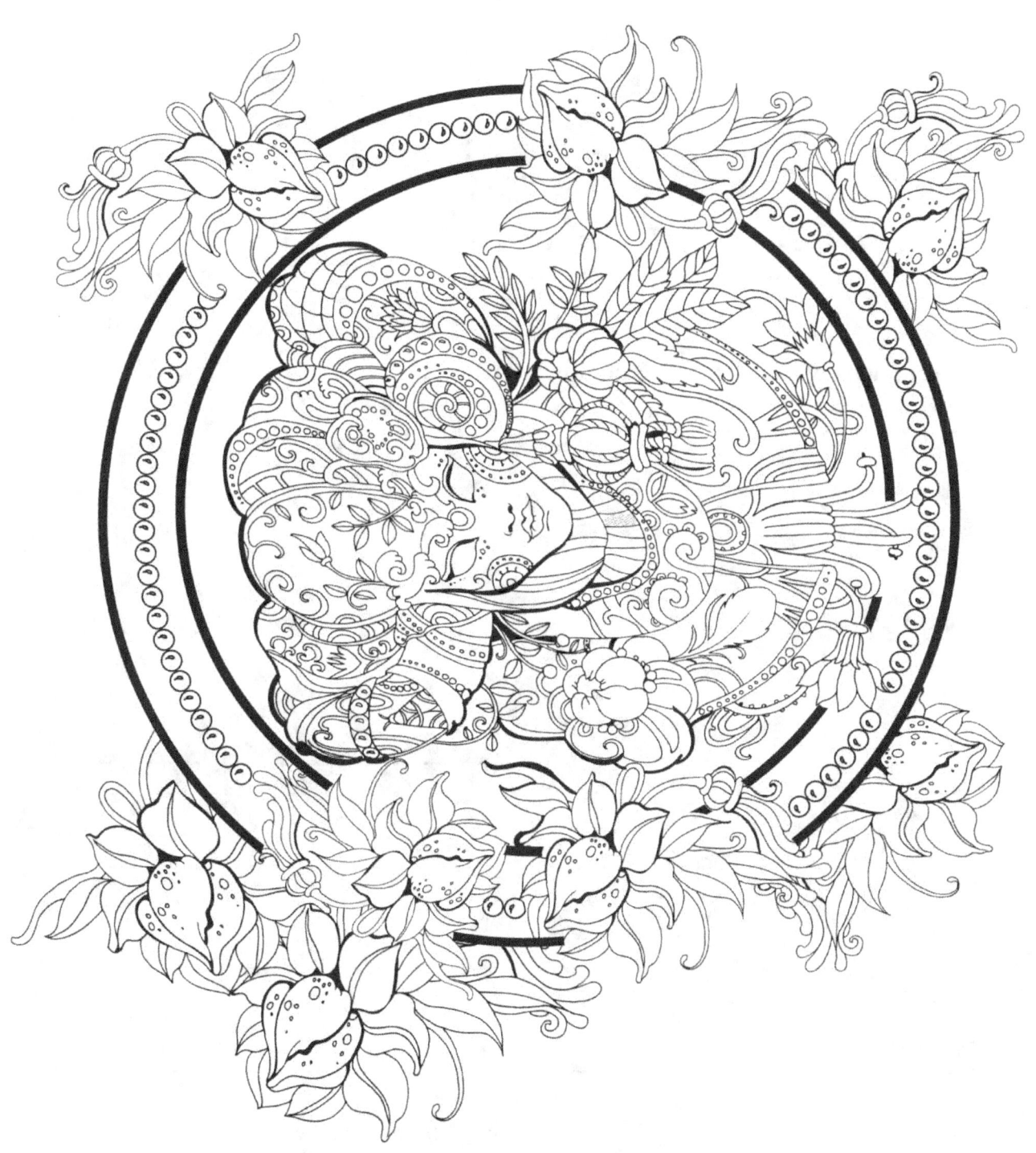

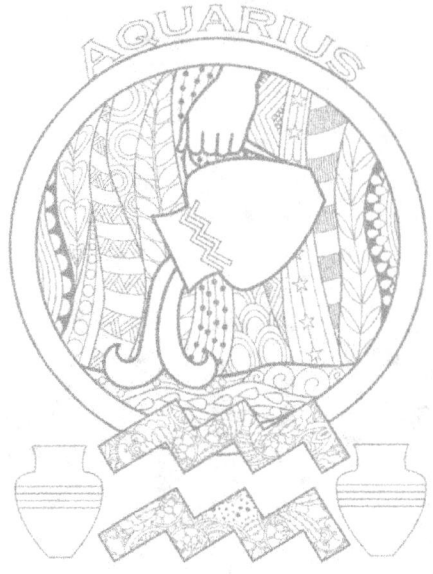

Aquarians will seek involvement in humanitarian causes.

_____

_____

_____

_____

_____

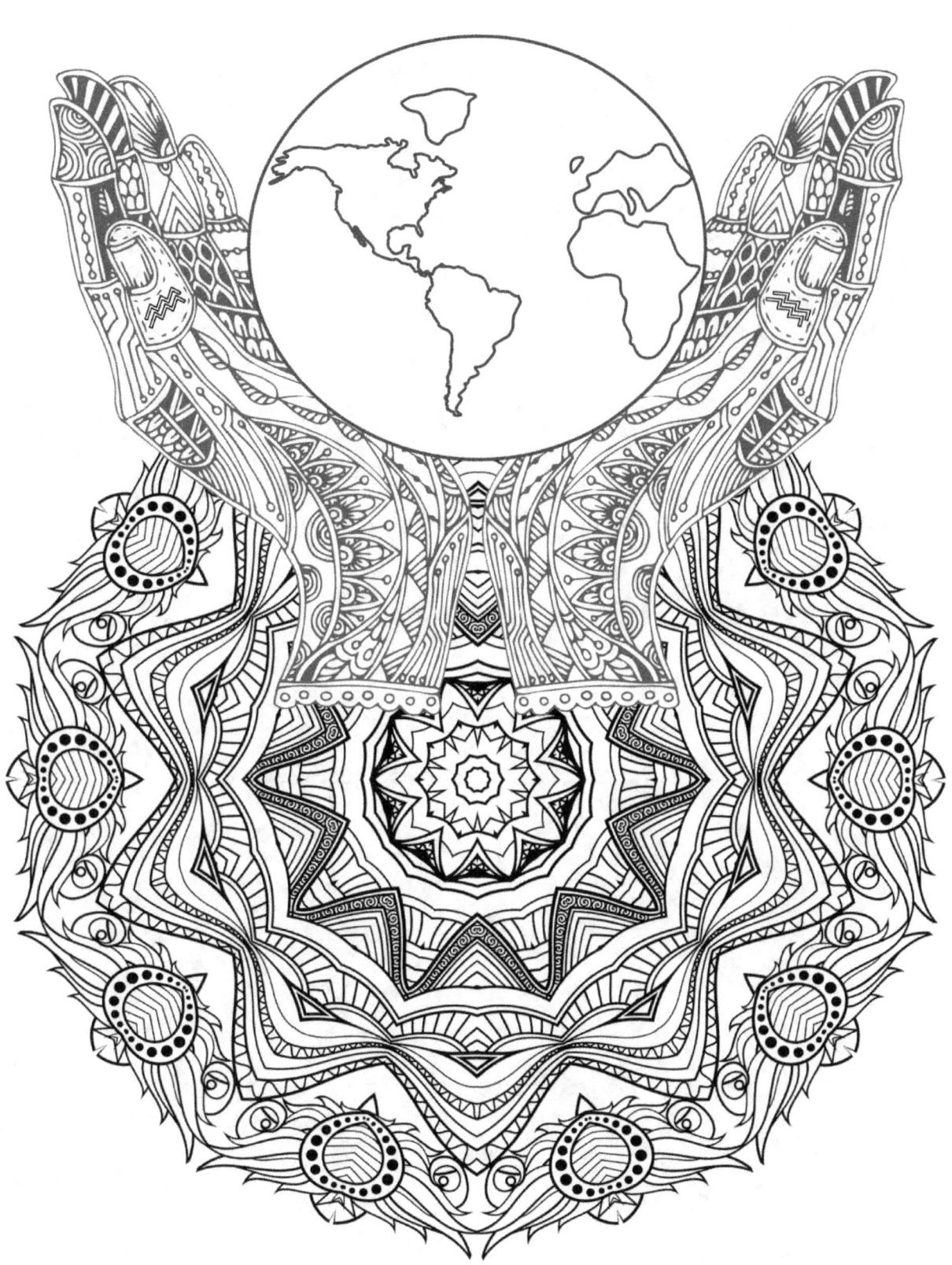

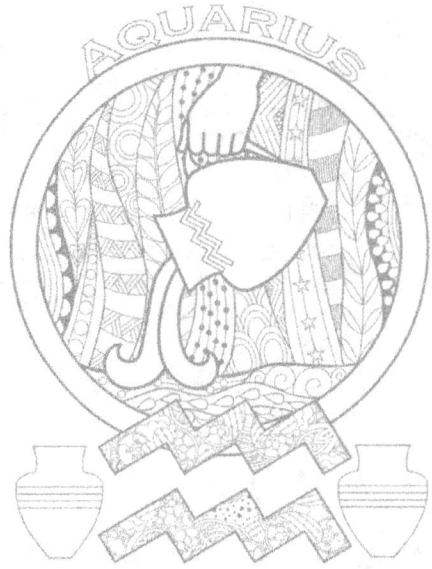

With their ability to come up with original ideas, Aquarians make good musicians.

_____

_____

_____

_____

_____

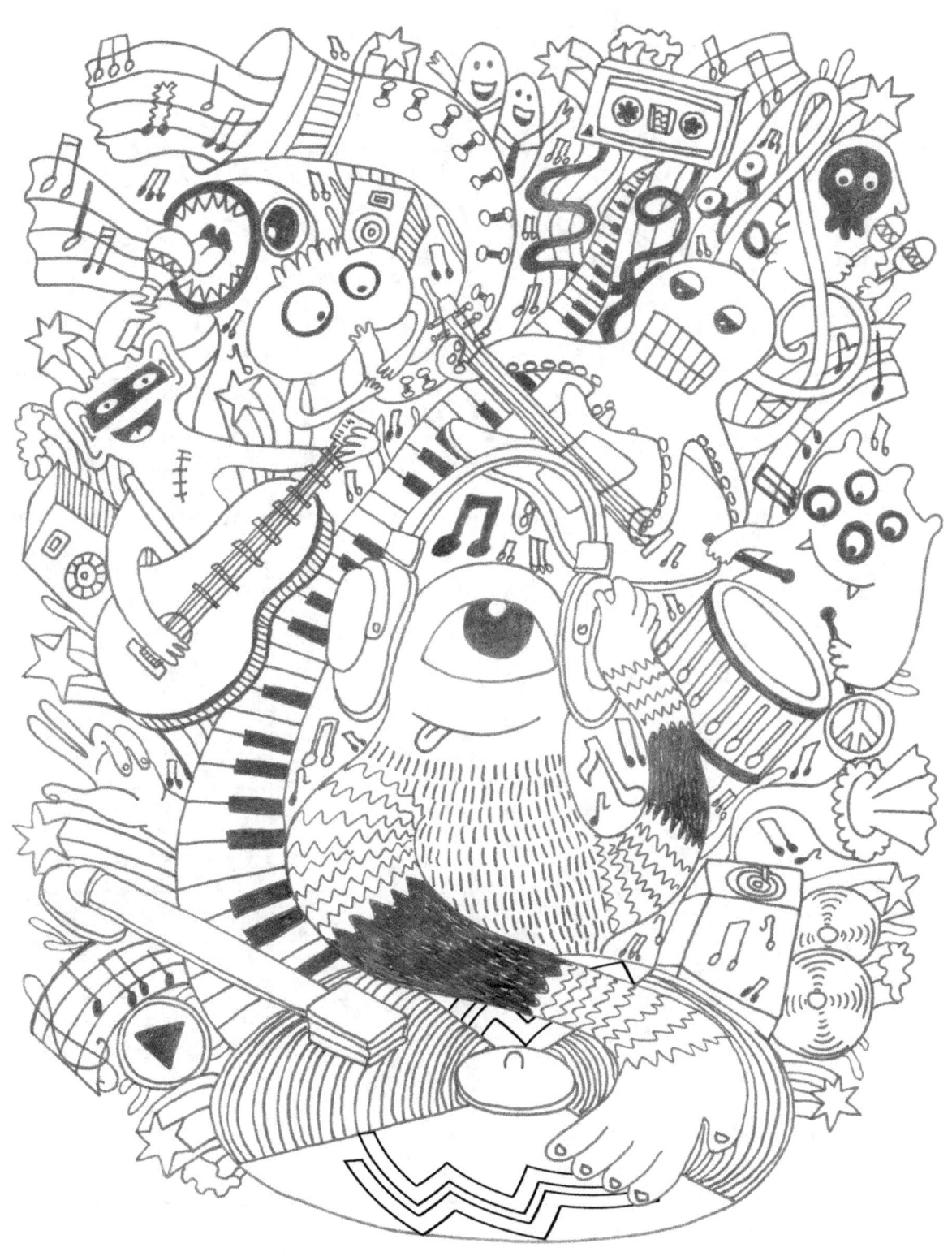

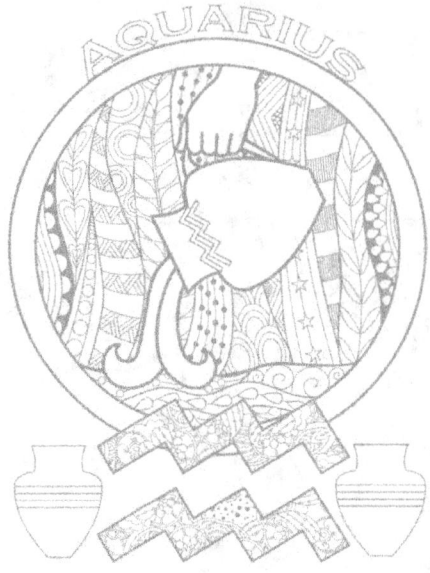

If you like throwing parties, have a surprise party for an Aquarian. They love surprises.

_____

_____

_____

_____

_____

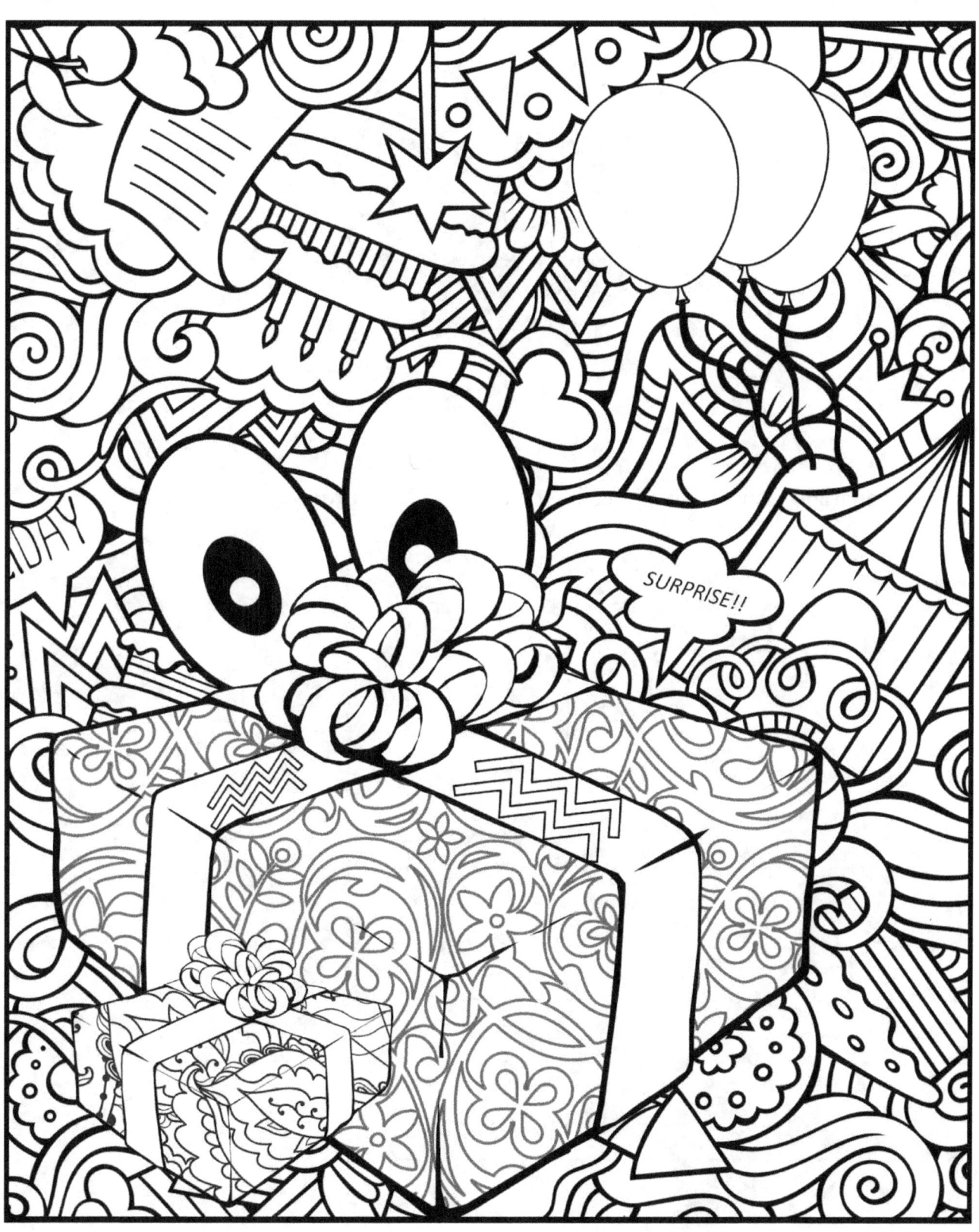

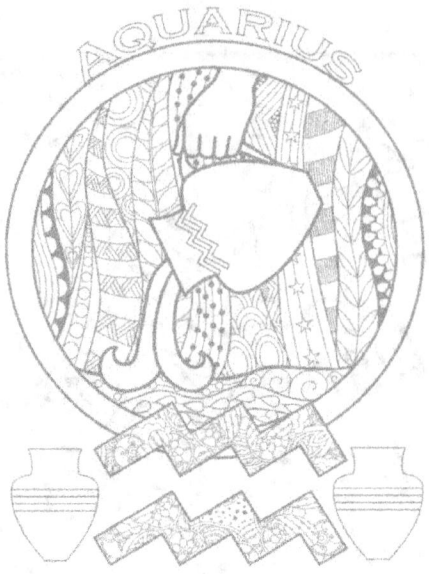

Aquarians usually have a feeling of unity with nature.

_____

_____

_____

_____

_____

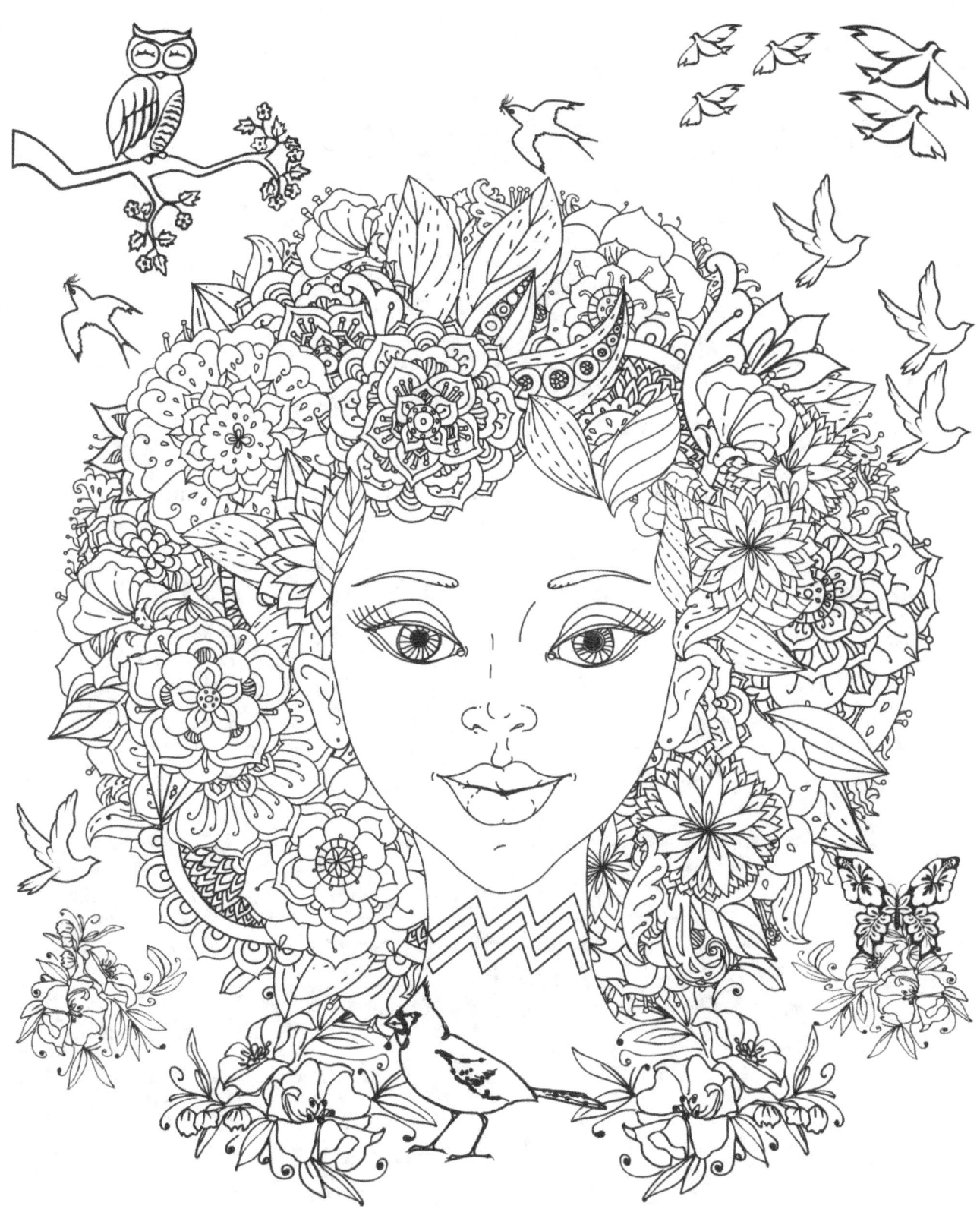

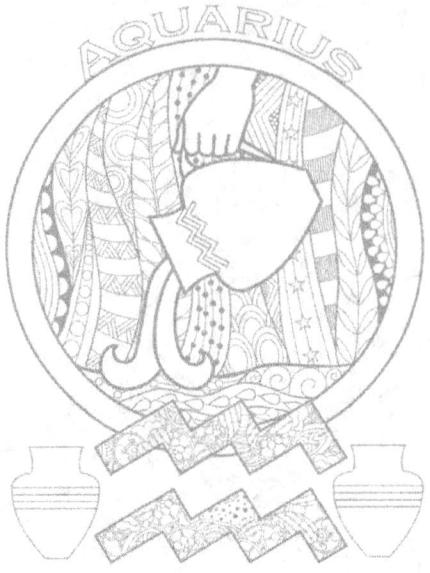

With Uranus as their ruler, Aquarians often put their energy into improving the world.

_____

_____

_____

_____

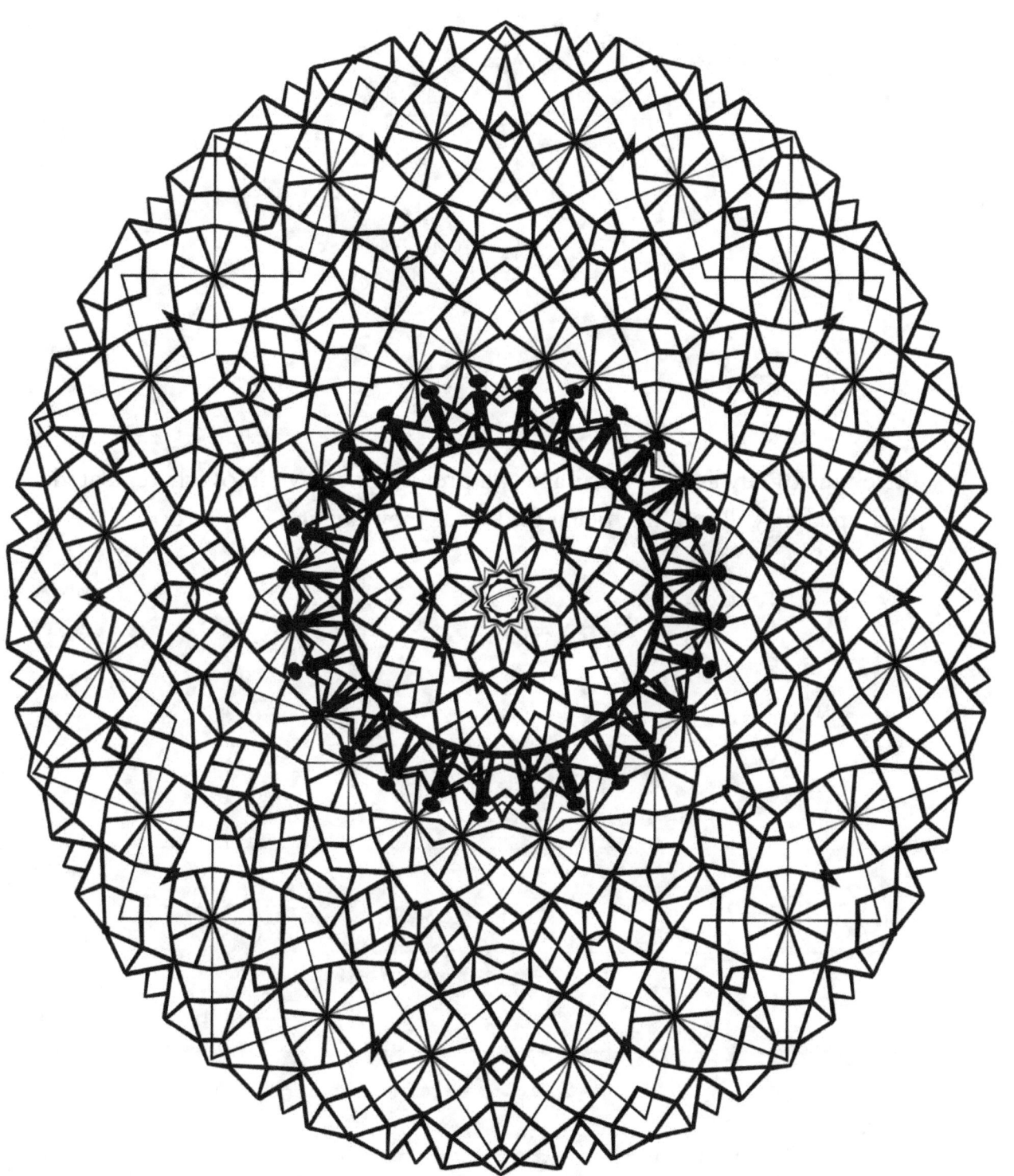

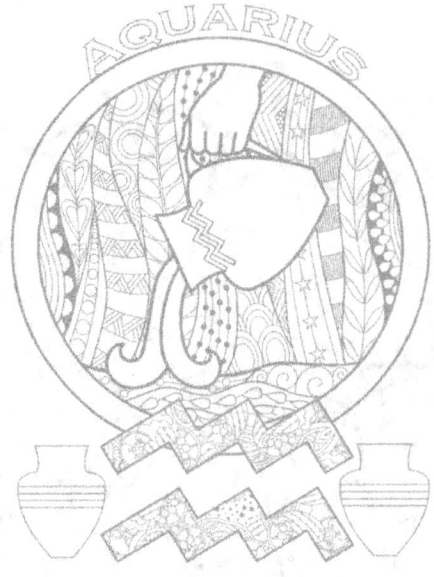

While fans of city living, Aquarians still prefer not to live in overly regulated areas since they do not like being told what they can and cannot do.

_____

_____

_____

_____

_____

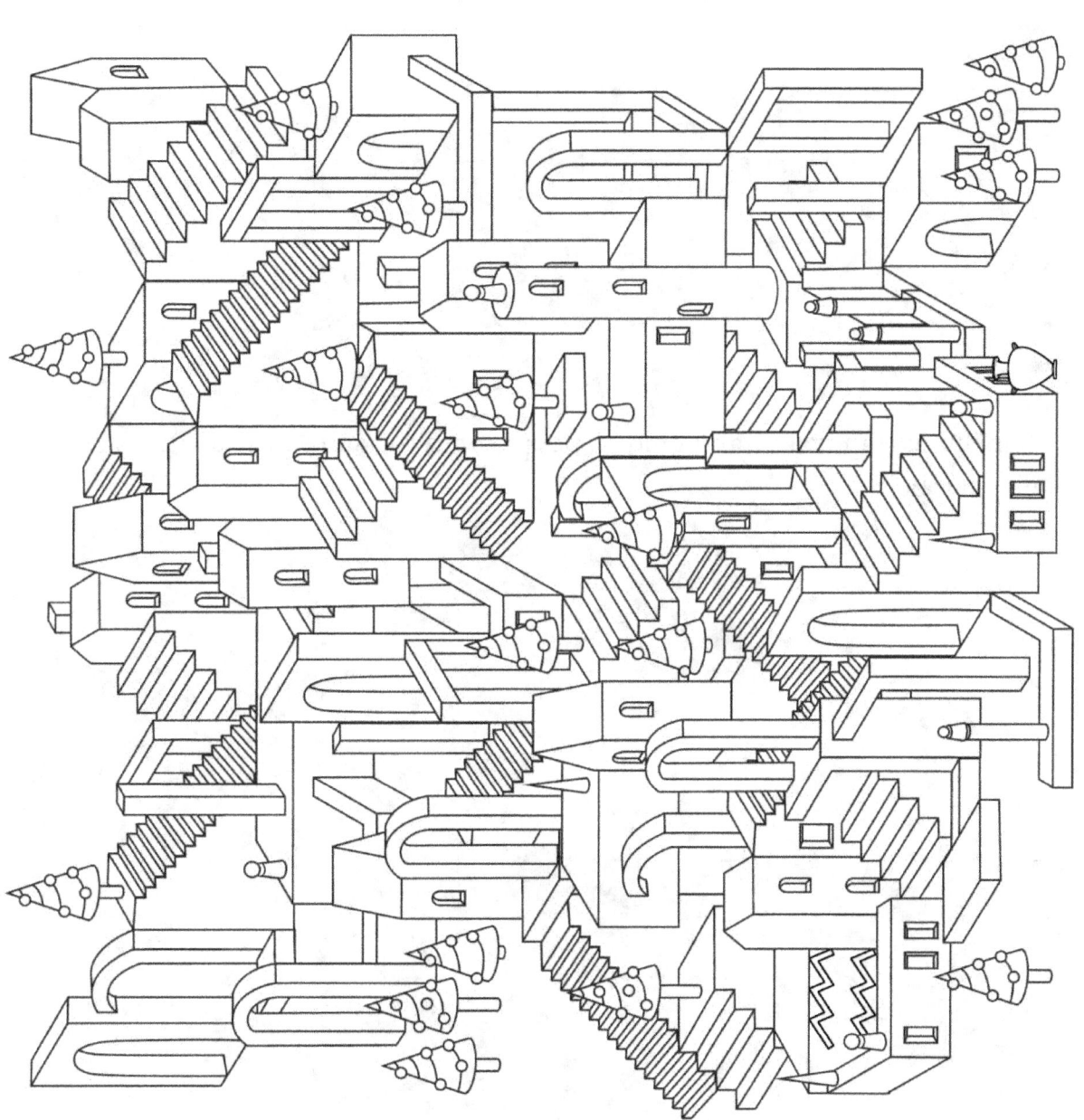

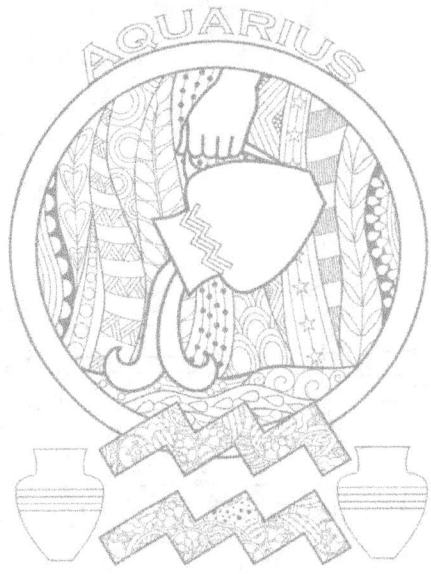

Rebellious, innovative and unique, people with the sun sign Aquarius are an exciting bunch.

_____

_____

_____

_____

_____

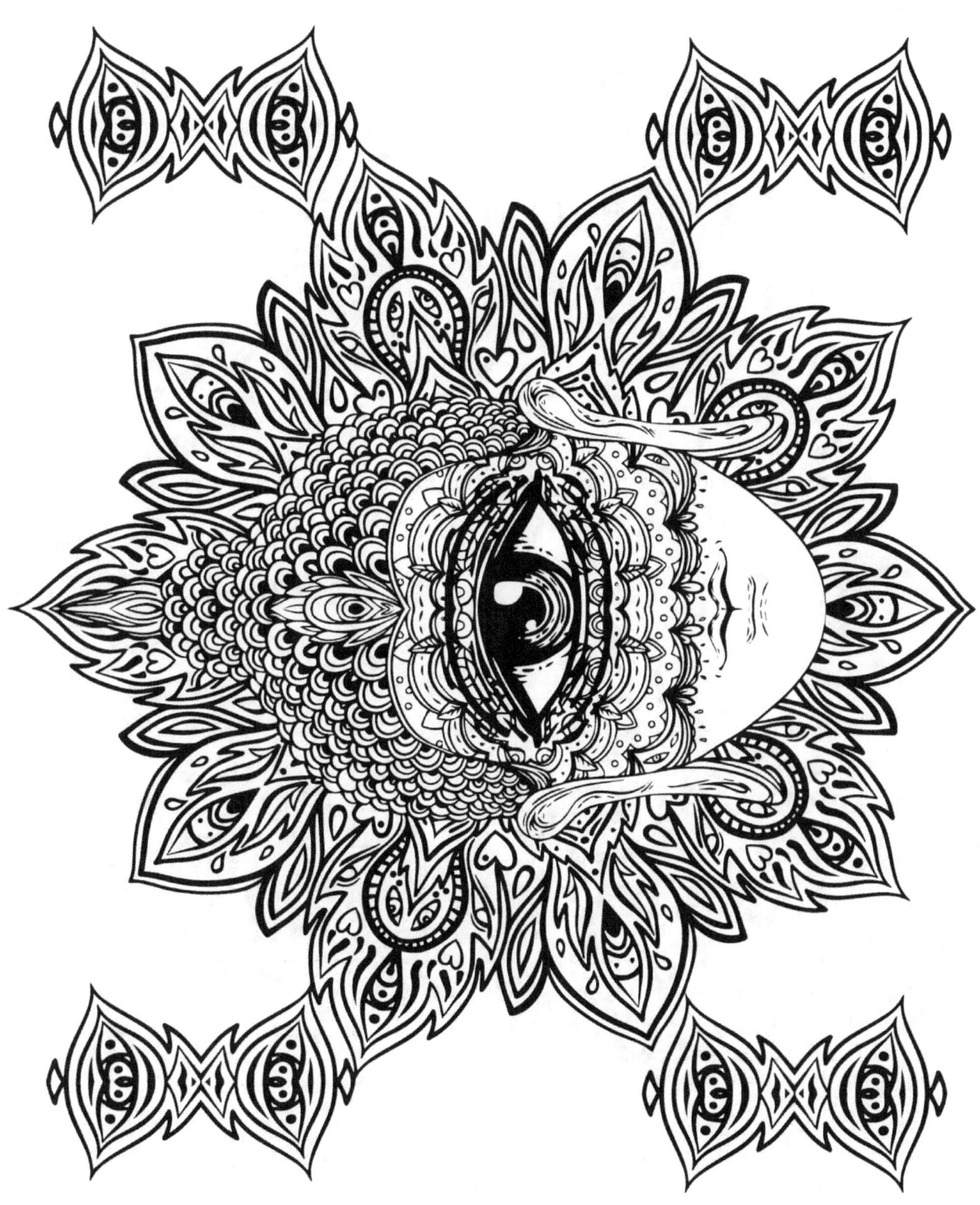

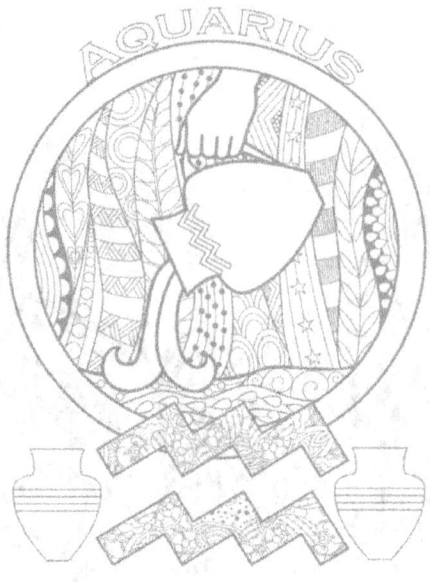

Loyalty in friends and partners is important to Aquarians and they will return it.

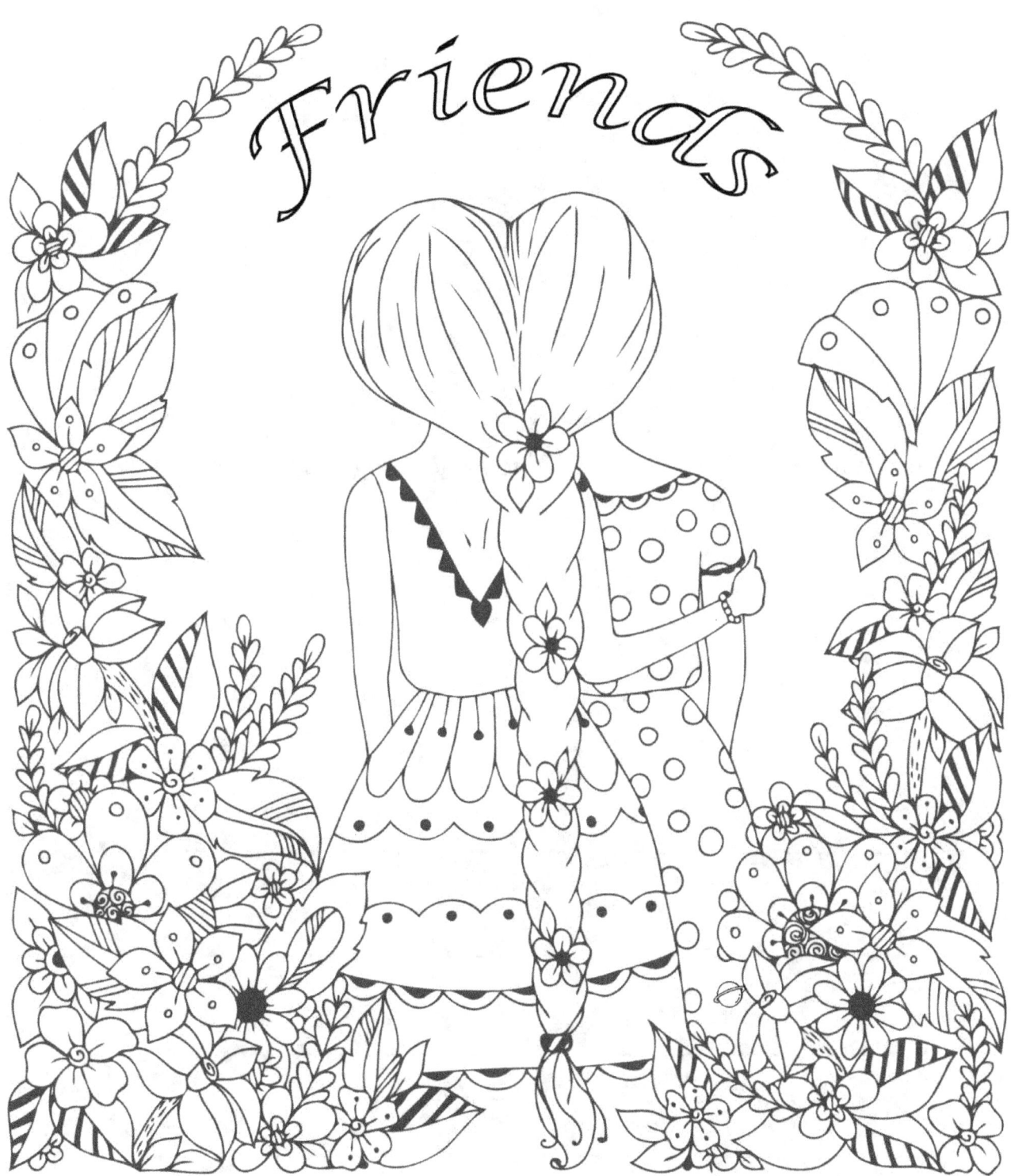

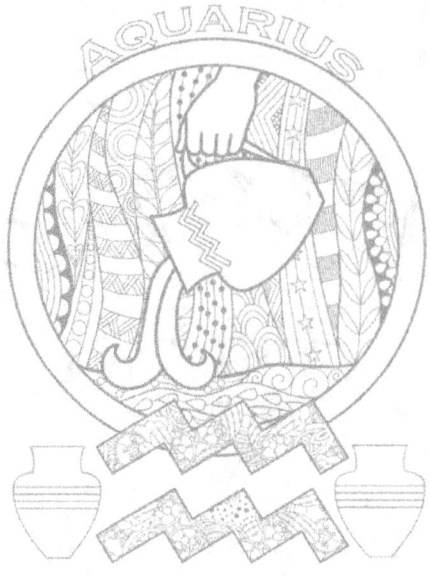

As an air sign, Aquarians are drawn to parachuting and ballooning.

_____

_____

_____

_____

_____

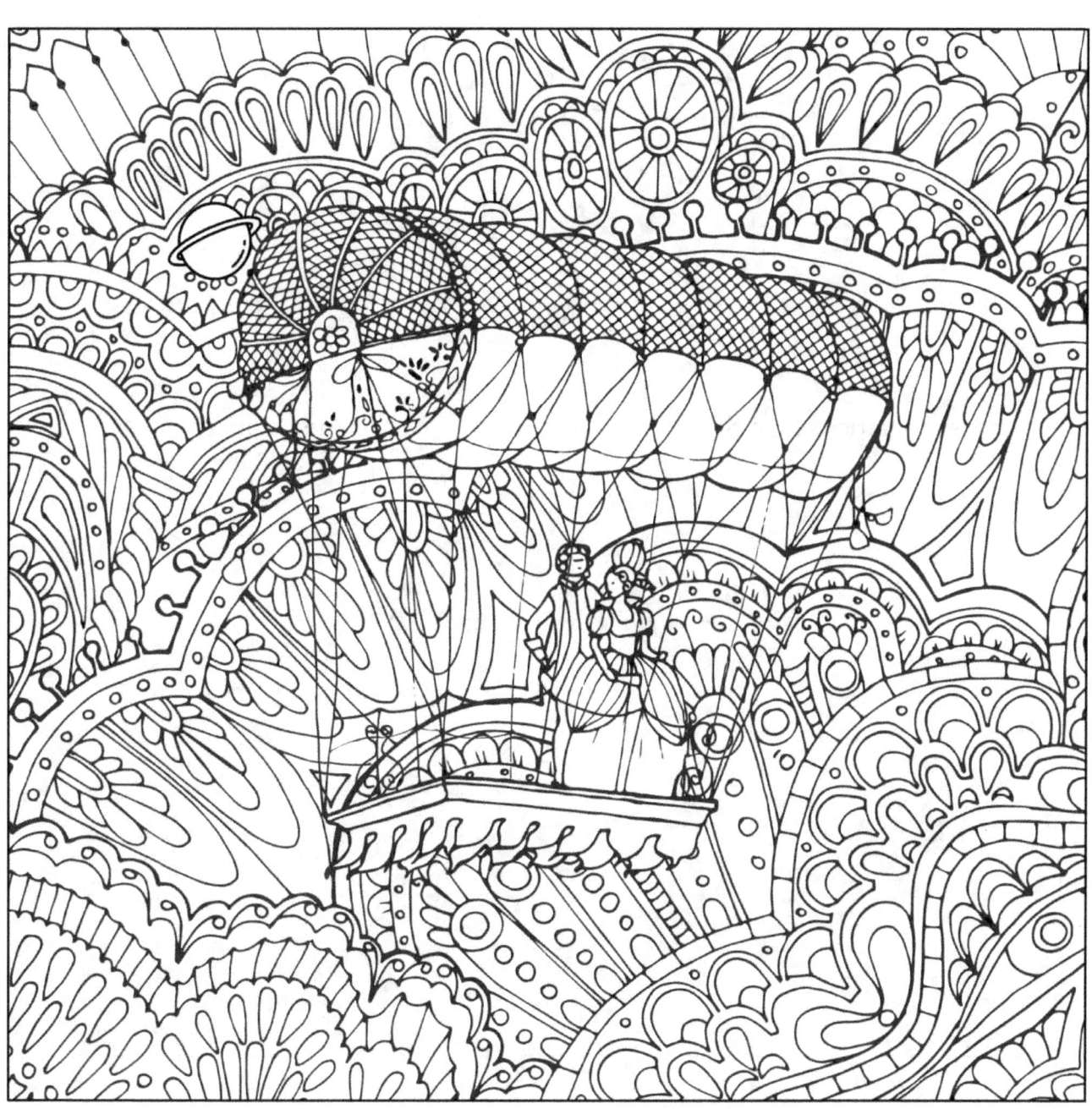

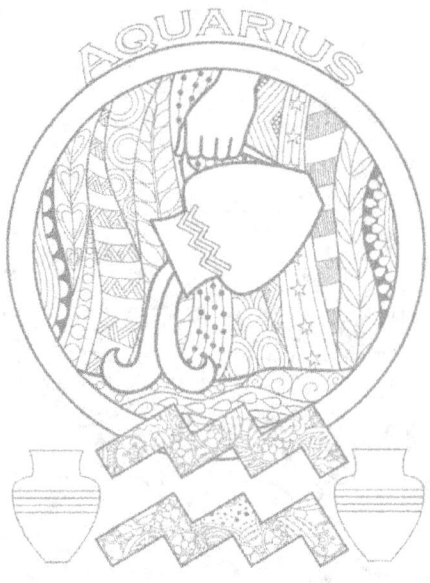

Most Aquarians love flip flops, especially ones out of the ordinary.

_____

_____

_____

_____

_____

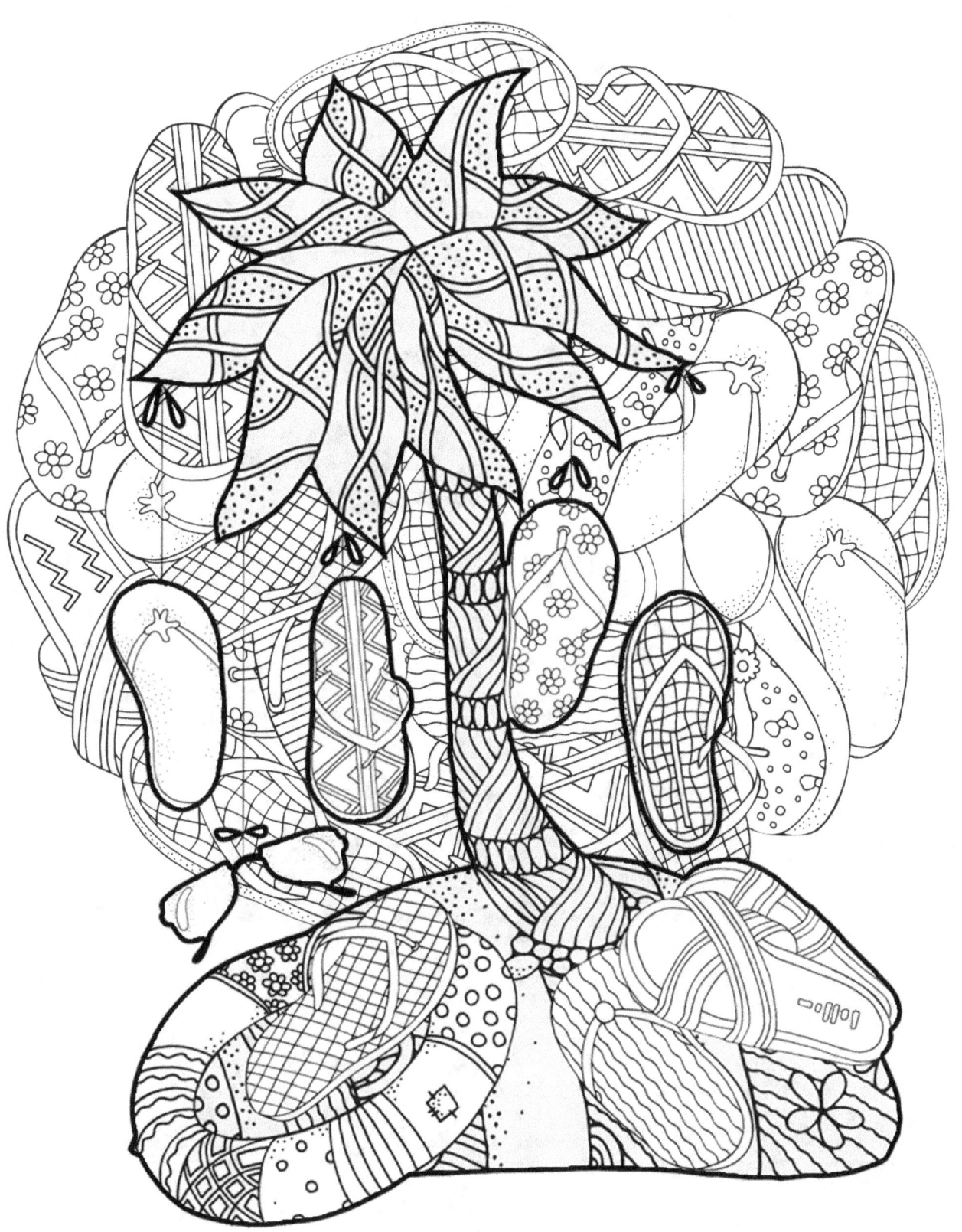

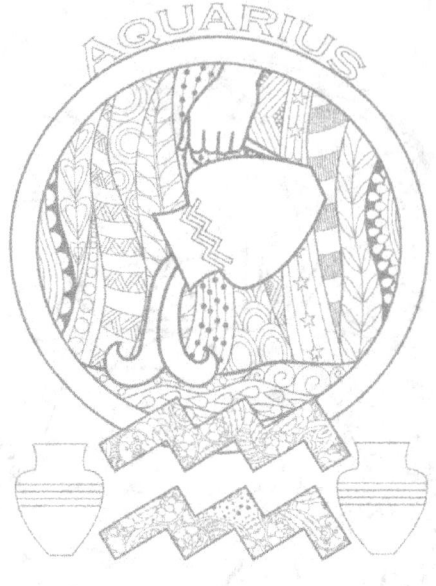

With their love of technology, Aquarians enjoy gaming.

_____

_____

_____

_____

_____

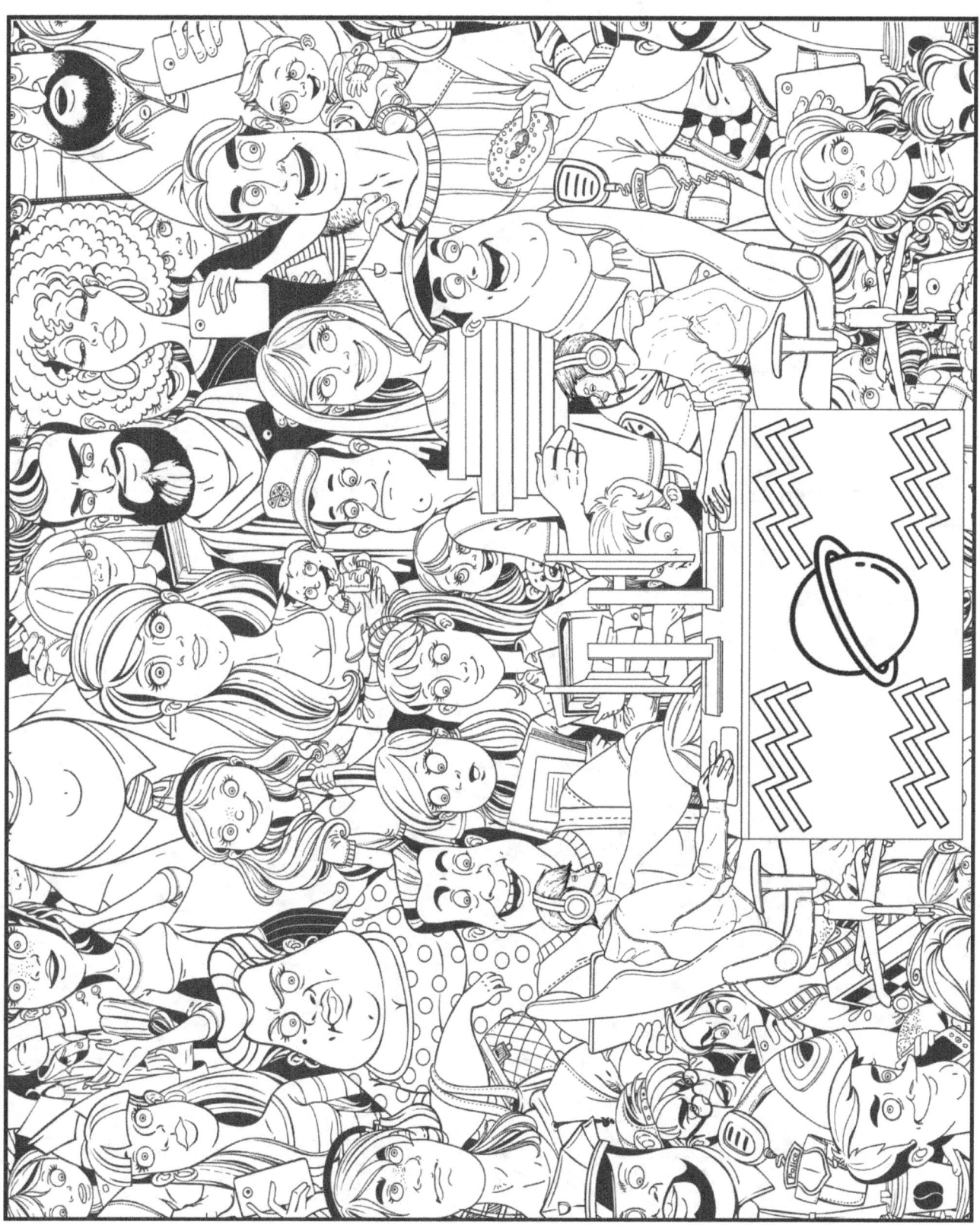

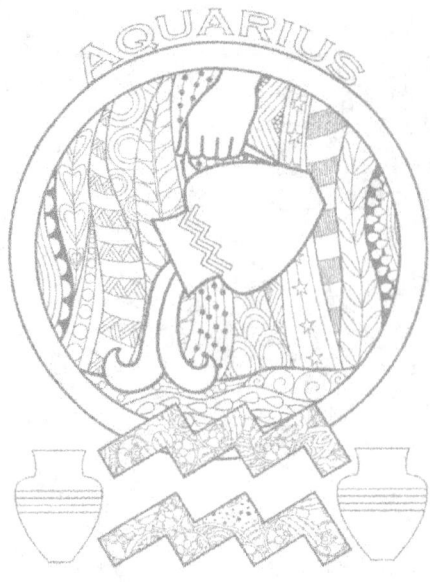

It has been said that a hamster would be a good choice for an Aquarius' pet.

_____

_____

_____

_____

_____

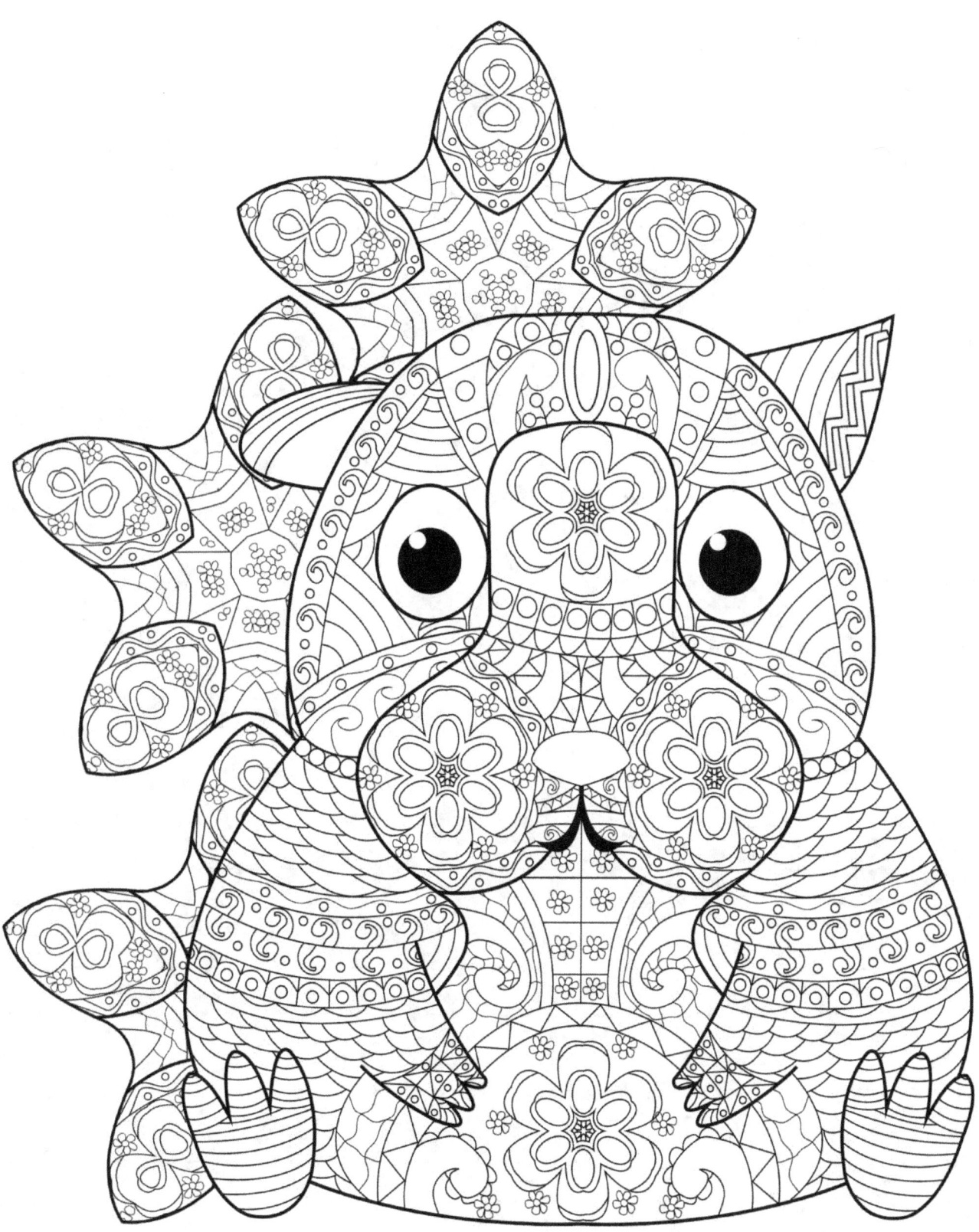

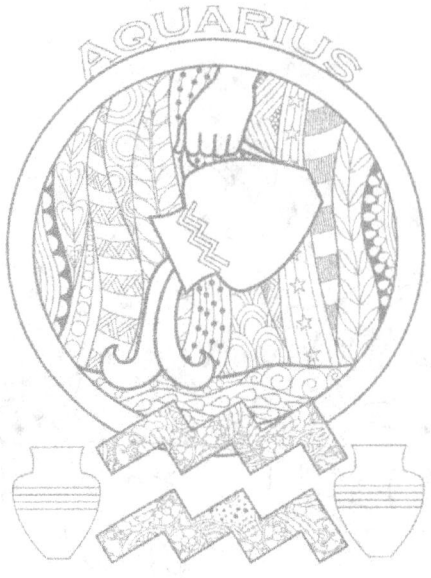

Aquarius Mandala - Uranus, Air, Kiwi, Water Jug, Amaryllis

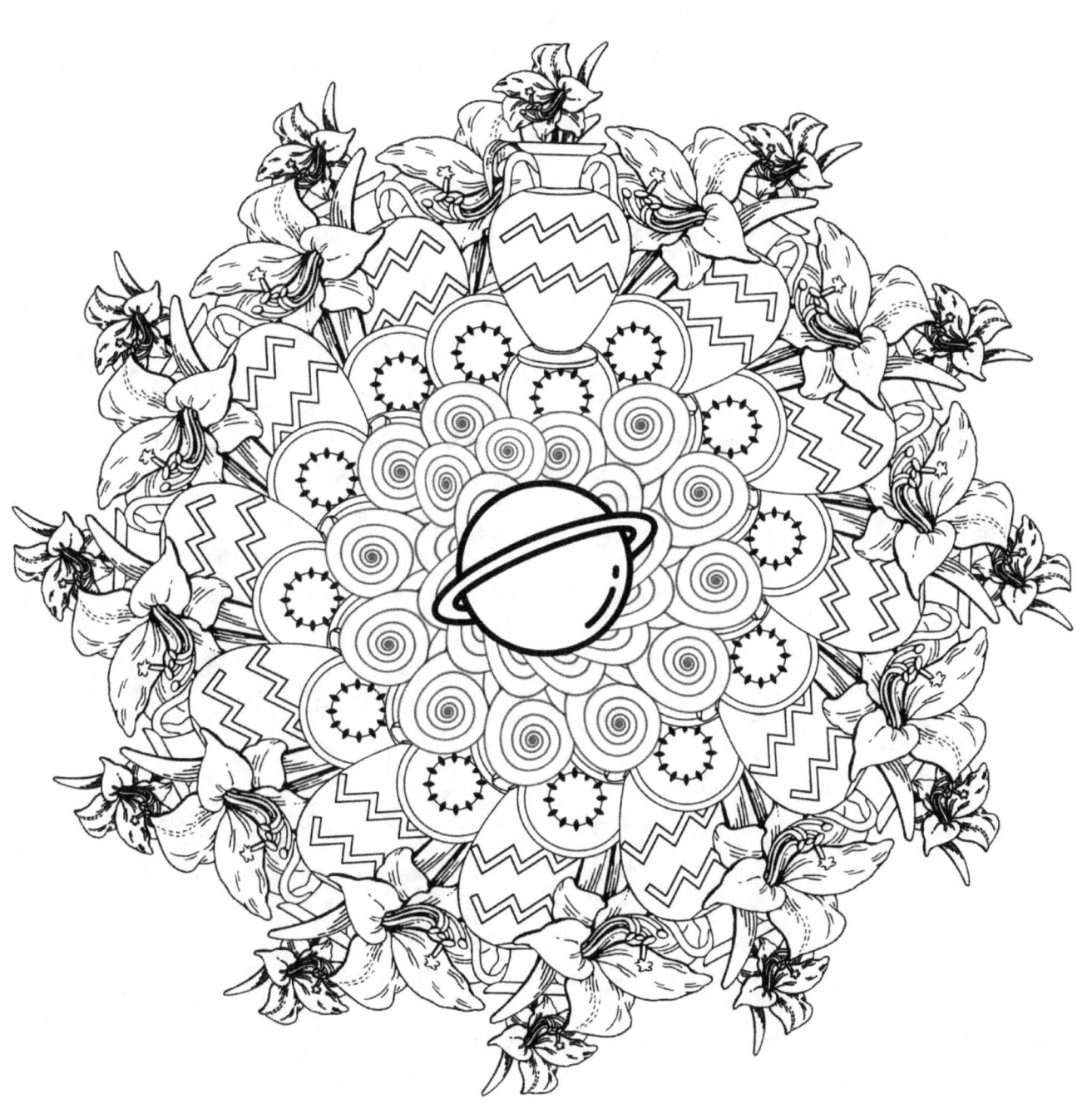

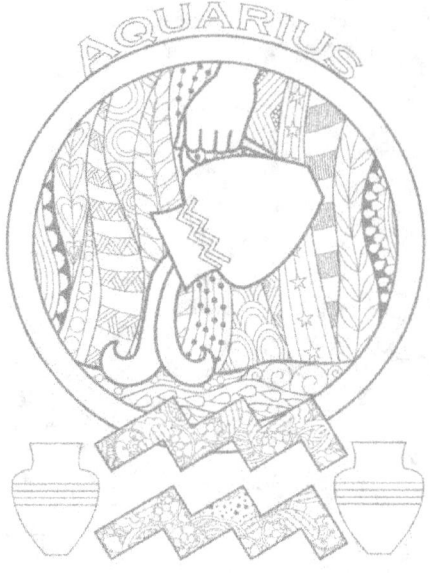

The water bearer is symbolic of the Gods nourishing the earth with life giving energies.

_____

_____

_____

_____

_____

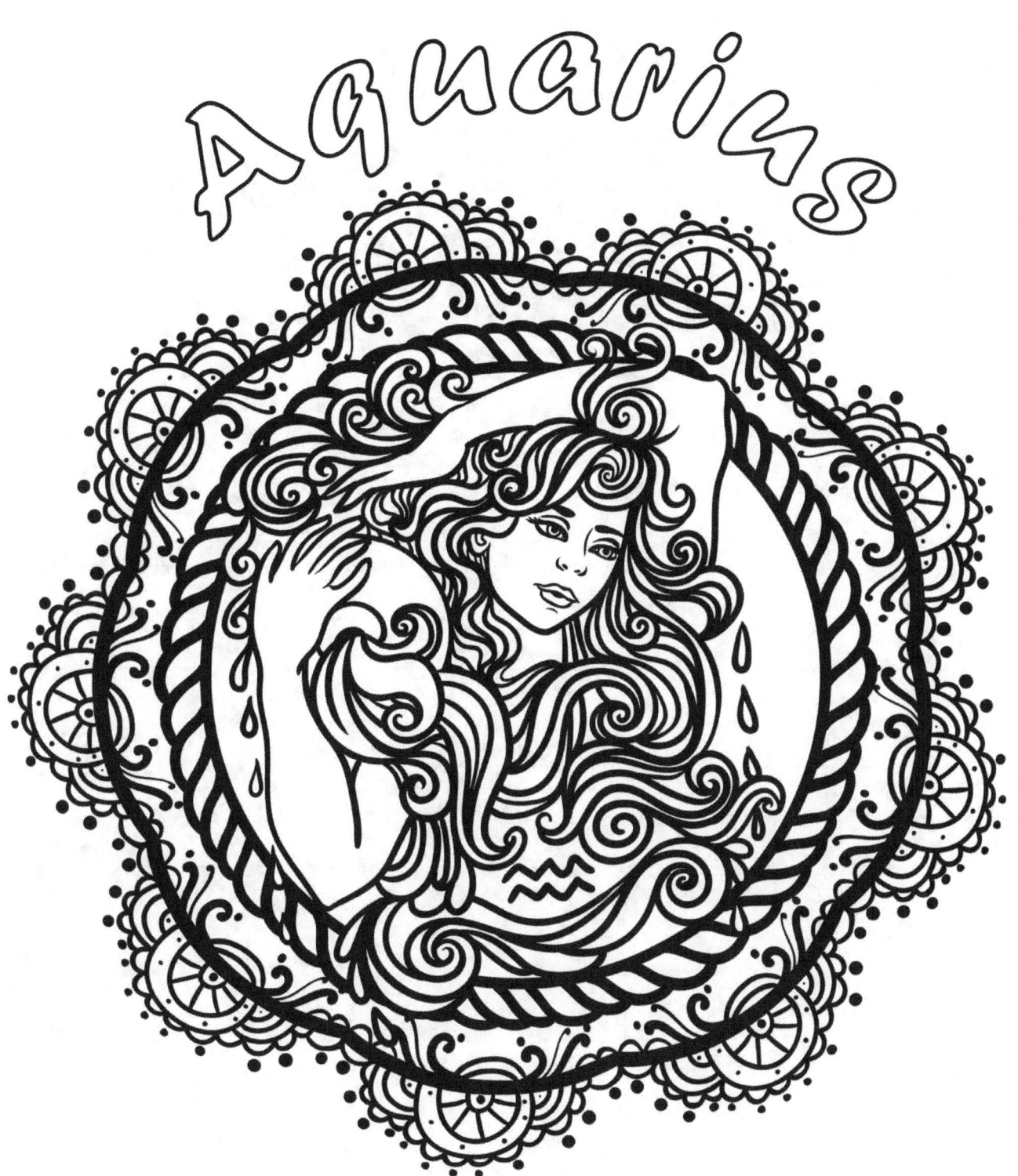

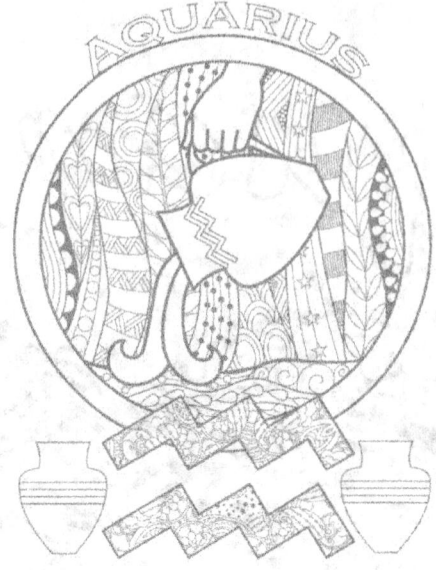

_____

_____

_____

_____

_____

SPECIAL DISCOUNT!

Many customers would like to color some of the coloring pages more than once. If you're one of them we have something special to share with you…

You can get the downloadable pdf version of this book at a special discount because you have purchased this book. You can download the book and print any coloring page as many times as you would like.

To take advantage of this offer simply:

1. Go to the product page:
   https://mytimetocolor.com/aquariuspdf
2. Add the pdf version to your cart
3. Click on Checkout (cart icon)
4. Enter the coupon code: pdf11za
5. Complete Checkout
6. **Download book and print your favourites!**

CONNECT WITH US!

We'd love to connect with you so please visit the website or like us on Facebook!

Website:

www.MyTimeToColor.com

Facebook:

http://Facebook.com/mytimetocolor

POST A REVIEW

Your review means a lot so please consider taking a moment and posting a review where you purchased this book. Thanks!!